Life After Death

Fact or Fiction?

Life After Death

Fact or Fiction?

Other books in the Fact or Fiction? series:

Life After Death

Fact or Fiction?

Kimberly Benton, *Book Editor*

Daniel Leone, *President*
Bonnie Szumski, *Publisher*
Scott Barbour, *Managing Editor*

OPPOSING
VIEWPOINTS®
SERIES

GREENHAVEN
PRESS®

THOMSON
━━━━━✶━━━━━ ™
GALE

San Diego • Detroit • New York • San Francisco • Cleveland
New Haven, Conn. • Waterville, Maine • London • Munich

THOMSON

GALE

© 2004 by Greenhaven Press. Greenhaven Press is an imprint of The Gale Group, Inc., a division of Thomson Learning, Inc.

Greenhaven® and Thomson Learning™ are trademarks used herein under license.

For more information, contact
Greenhaven Press
27500 Drake Rd.
Farmington Hills, MI 48331-3535
Or you can visit our Internet site at http://www.gale.com

Cover credit: The Image Bank

LIBRARY OF CONGRESS CATALOGING-IN-PUBLICATION DATA
Life after death / Kimberly Benton, book editor.
p. cm. — (Fact or fiction?)
Includes bibliographical references and index.
ISBN 0-7377-1736-X (pbk. : alk. paper) — ISBN 0-7377-1735-1 (lib. : alk. paper)
1. Future life. I. Benton, Kimberly, 1968– . II. Fact or fiction? (Greenhaven Press)
BL535.L54   2004
129—dc21   2002045484

Printed in the United States of America

Contents

Foreword

"There are more things in heaven and earth, Horatio, than are dreamt of in your philosophy."
                              —William Shakespeare, *Hamlet*

"Extraordinary claims require extraordinary evidence."
                              —Carl Sagan, *The Demon-Haunted World*

Almost every one of us has experienced something that we thought seemed mysterious and unexplainable. For example, have you ever known that someone was going to call you just before the phone rang? Or perhaps you have had a dream about something that later came true. Some people think these occurrences are signs of the paranormal. Others explain them as merely coincidence.

As the examples above show, mysteries of the paranormal ("beyond the normal") are common. For example, most towns have at least one place where inhabitants believe ghosts live. People report seeing strange lights in the sky that they believe are the spaceships of visitors from other planets. And scientists have been working for decades to discover the truth about sightings of mysterious creatures like Bigfoot and the Loch Ness monster.

There are also mysteries of magic and miracles. The two often share a connection. Many forms of magical belief are tied to religious belief. For example, many of the rituals and beliefs of the voodoo religion are viewed by outsiders as magical practices. These include such things as the alleged Haitian voodoo practice of turning people into zombies (the walking dead).

There are mysteries of history—events and places that have been recorded in history but that we still have questions about today. For example, was the great King Arthur a real king or merely a legend? How, exactly, were the pyramids built? Historians continue to seek the answers to these questions.

Then, of course, there are mysteries of science. One such mystery is how humanity began. Although most scientists agree that it was through the long, slow process of evolution, not all scientists agree that indisputable proof has been found.

Subjects like these are fascinating, in part because we do not know the whole truth about them. They are mysteries. And they are controversial—people hold very strong and opposing views about them.

How we go about sifting through information on such topics is the subject of every book in the Greenhaven Press series Fact or Fiction? Each anthology includes articles that present the main ideas favoring and challenging a given topic. The editor collects such material from a variety of sources, including scientific research, eyewitness accounts, and government reports. In addition, a final chapter gives readers tools to analyze the articles they read. With these tools, readers can sift through the information presented in the articles by applying the methods of hypothetical reasoning. Examining these topics in this way adds a unique aspect to the Fact or Fiction? series. Hypothetical reasoning can be applied to any topic to allow a reader to become more analytical about the material he or she encounters. While such reasoning may not solve the mystery of who is right or who is wrong, it can help the reader separate valid from invalid evidence relating to all topics and can be especially helpful in analyzing material where people disagree.

Introduction

People have always been fascinated with life after death. Every religion, for example, answers the question, "What happens to us after we die?" A major difference for Americans is that people previously obtained their information, comfort, and beliefs from their traditional religious teachings. Today it is more common for Americans to seek alternative avenues when exploring information about life after death. While a 1999 Gallup poll found that only 13 percent of Americans today attend weekly church service, books, movies, television, and professions that deal with the topic of life after death are on the increase.

Professional Guidance

Although traditional religion is still a factor in molding America's belief system in matters of life after death, more Americans today are investigating alternative views. In addition to the clergy, psychologists, physicians, and psychics are becoming more mainstream as sources of information about the afterlife. Today it is common practice to seek counseling about life, death, and the afterlife. Patients seek out psychiatrists who use hypnotherapy and dream interpretation to help clients explore past lives. Patients are also seeking doctors that are experts in near-death experiences (NDEs). Scientifically, more is being learned about what happens after death.

The increased interest in alternative beliefs may be sparked by greater scientific exploration into the topic of life after death. The field of psychology commonly recognizes hypnosis, NDEs, and dreams as legitimate scientific areas that explore life after death. There are even degreed programs from universities that offer classes in the paranormal. For example, Breyer State University, an online university, offers degrees in metaphysics and spiritual counseling. Examples of course work include angelology, mediumship and spiritual counseling, and psychic development.

Hypnosis

One growing area that explores life after death is hypnosis. Many people believe that through hypnosis they can recall past-life information, also known as past-life regression. Psychiatrists and others trained in hypnosis attempt to help the patient by tapping into his or her subconscious mind. "Hypnosis involves a very deep relaxation process that allows the brainwaves to slow down into the alpha or theta range. Within these brainwave frequencies, our memory and recall are greatly enhanced."[1] This therapy is used to help patients correct their mistakes in this life, to discover hidden talents from prior lives, and to understand their current problems. People explore the possibilities that what happens after death is simply another life. These people believe that life and death are a continuous progression.

Hypnotists trained in exploring these matters are becoming more available to the public. Because degrees are offered in many areas of hypnosis, this field is no longer limited to doctors and psychologists. For example, Gary Nurkiewicz is a past-life regression counselor. Nurkiewicz offers classes, workshops, and lectures and also has a private practice in Denver, Colorado. Nurkiewicz is board certified in many areas of hypnosis, including past-life regression, even though he is not a licensed psychologist. Patients are willing to pay Nurkiewicz $175 for a one-hour session on past-life regression.

The most common reason people turn to past-life regression is to understand their own life better by understanding what happened to them in past lives. Helen Wambach has made it her life's work to research people's experiences with past-life regression. As a trained hypnotist, she has spent years exploring what she believes are her clients' vivid memories of past lives. One of her subjects remembered a life believed to have been lived in A.D. 25.

> The map was somewhere in northern Italy around the Adriatic Sea. I lived in a stone village. The houses were quite clear to me. They were one-story, with low doorways. When I went to the marketplace, I bought grain and some kind of tool that I must have used in my woodworking business. . . . I ate with other men at the table. They didn't seem to be related to me; it was as though somehow we all worked together or lived together. I had the feeling that my family was somewhere in the countryside and that I worked in this village. The coin I used to buy my supplies is interesting. Actually, I had two coins. One of them was a dark gray and had a hole in the middle. It seemed to be shaped like a square with the corners pounded to try to make it look round.[2]

The coin was later identified as one common to that period in time. Wambach believes that the accuracy of historical information given to her from patients under hypnosis proves that the soul travels from one life to the next.

Dreams

Many Americans believe that dreams are evidence of an afterlife. Today, the ancient Egyptian belief that dreams were a window into the afterlife is being revived. The Egyptians believed that they could view activities of a deceased loved one through their dreams. This convinced them of an afterlife, and they therefore did not view death as the end but as a passage into an eternal life.

People are seeking dream analysts to help them understand how their dreams relate to death and how dreams prove an afterlife. Claire Sylvia believes her dreams connect her to the afterlife. Sylvia was dying, in need of a heart and lung transplant, when she began having strange dreams that were confusing to her:

> I'm in an open field and it's very light. It's daytime and I'm in a playful relationship with a young man whom I see clearly. He is tall, has sandy colored hair and his name is Tim L. I come back and say goodbye to him and as we approach each other, we kiss, as we kiss, I feel as if I inhale him into me. It's like taking this enormous breath. And I know that he will be with me together forever. But it also seemed that this man in my dreams, who I knew as Tim, must be my donor.[3]

Immediately following her heart transplant, she began experiencing new sensations that were also confusing, such as a sudden liking to green peppers. Eventually she learned that she had been dreaming about her heart donor. She believes he was communicating with her through her dreams. This type of dreaming, termed after-death communication (ADC) has happened to many others.

Bill and Judy Guggenheim are credited as the first to conduct an in-depth study of ADCs. They interviewed two thousand people and recorded over three hundred dreams believed to be ADCs. They found through their research that ADCs are different than ordinary dreams:

> There are many significant differences between an ordinary dream and a sleep-state ADC. A dream is generally fragmented, jumbled, filled with symbolism, and incomplete in various ways. In contrast, sleep-state ADCs feel like actual face-to-face visits with deceased loved ones. They are much more orderly, colorful, vivid, and memorable than most dreams.[4]

The Guggenheims estimate that as many as 50 million people have experienced an ADC. Psychotherapists today are using the idea of ADCs to help grieving people reconnect with deceased loved ones. Psychotherapist Dr. Allan

Boutin reports that patients who experience an ADC resolve "the grief and pain of traumatic loss quickly, easily, and permanently."[5] Boutin and others believe ADC is no hallucination, instead that it is a direct connection to someone who has died. Boutin believes this proves life exists after death.

NDEs

Physicians today play an important role in helping people understand life after death. Not only do they help prepare those about to die, but they are also leaders in field research on NDEs. Melvin Morse, for example, is a pediatrician and a neuroscientist who has researched the NDEs of children for fifteen years. Morse believes that people have an underused area of their brain that controls spiritual intuitions and paranormal abilities. This area of the brain is called on at the time near death, which makes death a pleasurable, not fearful, experience. Morse is currently working on a manual that will teach people how to utilize the area of the brain that is linked to NDEs to better understand a person's paranormal abilities.

Morse began his work when taking care of Katie, a nine-year-old who had to be resuscitated after nearly drowning. While unconscious, Katie had what was later called a near-death experience. After waking, Katie reported to Morse that she visited Jesus and the Heavenly Father. She said she was escorted through a tunnel by a girl named Elisabeth and greeted by her late grandfather. She was allowed to visit her house and observe her family. When she met Jesus, he asked her if she wanted to see her family again. When she said yes, she woke out of her coma. One startling discovery was that Katie's family did not have a strong religious foundation; Morse concluded that Katie's memory was real and not a learned religious response.

Morse's experience with Katie prompted him to do further

research and to publish his findings in a medical journal, arguably the first NDE account of a child. "I wanted other pediatricians to know that children had such experiences. My main motivation was to get doctors to contemplate the meaning of these experiences so they could help patients understand the dying process. I thought nothing could be more universal than the psychological events of dying."[6]

Morse is not alone in his conclusions. One recent poll estimated that 8 million Americans have experienced an NDE. Most have also reported feeling comforted by their experience, some changing their beliefs in the afterlife. In one survey on the aftereffects of NDEs, 38 percent felt more spiritual, 42 percent felt more joy, and 30 percent felt peace. Only 10 percent reported feeling a sense of loss. Half of those polled said they are now convinced of life after death.

Psychics

Hiring a psychic to find out about a deceased loved one is another way that people choose to explore life after death. A 1996 Gallup poll found that 20 percent of those polled believed that the dead could contact the living. Consulting a psychic medium is one of the fastest-growing trends in searching for answers to the afterlife. A psychic medium contacts the dead, reassuring people their deceased loved ones are safe. Psychic John Edward, for example, has played a significant role in the increased popularity in psychics. In fact, Edward may be the most profitable psychic to date. He has three books and one audio program currently in circulation; two of his books reached the *New York Times* best-seller list. His most recent book, *Crossing Over*, spent nine weeks on the *New York Times* best-seller list. The success of his books has led to appearances on talk shows, including NBC's *Today Show, Dateline, Larry King Live,* and *Live with Regis*.

People's interest in paranormal views on life after death

has grown so strong that more television programming is being set aside for the paranormal. The Sci-Fi Channel created a show for Edward, *Crossing Over*, which became the all-time top-rated show on the Sci-Fi Channel. In fact, it raised the Sci-Fi Channel ratings 33 percent in one year. Psychic James Van Praagh recently launched the *Beyond Show*, which is very similar to Edward's show. These shows have fueled beliefs that people live after death and long to communicate with the living.

New-Age Trends and America's Beliefs

Many of these new beliefs have culminated in actual religious and spiritual trends deemed "New Age." People who adhere to new-age beliefs have spawned the popularity of psychic fairs, modern-day séances, and new-age shops. There are also many phone consultation businesses and websites about spiritualism. Simply typing in the keywords *psychic hot line* brought 114,000 hits on the Internet. One example is kasamba.com, a site featuring several psychics offering live personal psychic readings ranging from one dollar to two dollars per minute. Users can choose to chat or interact via e-mail. Services were offered in counseling, numerology, astrology, and tarot readings.

Seminars on new-age beliefs are commonly held at new-age shops. They teach classes on dream interpretation, clairvoyance, how to be psychic, and other popular topics. For example, Fred Fassett offers weekly and monthly classes on an array of psychic techniques, including clairvoyance, past-life readings, tarot reading, and transmediumship. Prices range from twenty dollars to fifty-five dollars per session.

Psychic fairs are an excellent source of new-age information. Almost every major city holds regularly scheduled psychic fairs. This is a chance for all those in the psychic business to showcase their talents. All types of psychic readers are found at these venues, including tarot card readers, palm readers, acupuncturists, herbalists, and hypnotists. Cincinnati has been hosting a psychic fair since 1992, drawing nationally known presenters and thousands of visitors each year.

The Future

Most people agree there is some form of an afterlife. However, most disagree on what type of afterlife. The authors from the viewpoints that follow believe they have supported claims on their beliefs for or against an afterlife. They offer a wide range of expert opinions from many facets of life after death, including NDEs, psychic communications, religious viewpoints, reincarnation, and hypnosis.

Notes

1. *Passages Through Time: Past Life and Afterlife Regressions to Discover Your Soul's Purpose*, Subconscious-Solutions, 2002. www.passagesthroughtime.com.
2. Helen Wambach, *Reliving Past Lives: The Evidence Under Hypnosis*. New York: Barnes and Noble, 1978, pp. 100–101.
3. Kevin Williams, *The Secret World of Dreams: A Connection to the Afterlife*, Near-Death Experiences and the Afterlife, 2003. www.near-death.com.
4. Bill and Judith Guggenheim, *After-Death Communication: Joyous Reunions with Deceased Loved Ones*, The ADC Project, 2002. www.after-death.com.
5. Dr. Allan Botkin, *Induced ADC's*, Business Writing Center, 2002. http://inducedadc.com.
6. Melvin Morse and Paul Perry, *Closer to the Light: Learning from Children's Near-Death Experiences*. New York: Villard Books, 1990, pp. 12–13.

Chapter 1

Life After Death
Is a Fact

Near-Death Experiences Are Proof of Life After Death

Elisabeth Kübler-Ross

Near-death experiences or NDEs are one of the most common explanations of proof that there is life after death. Many nonbelievers have been quickly converted after having experienced an NDE. Dr. Elisabeth Kübler-Ross has devoted her life to working with dying patients. She began her career as a skeptic of life after death. However, years of witnessing people pass on have given her a great deal of insight into death, dying, and the afterlife. The following excerpt is from a lecture given by Kübler-Ross. She explains the process of near-death experiences and why it is proof of life after death.

I wanted to share with you some research on death and life after death. I think the time has come when we are all going to put these findings together in a language that can help people to understand, and also perhaps help them in dealing with, the death of a loved one. Especially the tragic occurrence of a sudden death when we don't quite understand why these tragedies have to happen to us. It is also very important when you try to counsel and help dying people and their families. And the question occurs over and over again, "What is life, what is death, and why do young children—especially young children—have to die?". . .

Awareness of Spirituality

A long time ago, people were much more in touch with the issue of death and believed in heaven or life after death. It is only in the last hundred years, perhaps, that fewer and fewer people truly know that life exists after the physical body dies. We are now in a new age, and hopefully we have made a transition from an age of science and technology and materialism to a new age of genuine and authentic spirituality. This does not mean religiosity, but rather, spirituality. Spirituality is an awareness that there is something far greater than we are, something that created this universe, created life, and that we are an authentic, important, significant part of it, and can contribute to its evolution.

All of us when we were born from the Source, from God, were endowed with a facet of divinity. That means, in a very literal sense, that we have a part of that source within us. That is what gives us the knowledge of our immortality. Many people are beginning to be aware that the physical body is only the house or the temple, or as we call it the cocoon, which we inhabit for a certain number of months or years until we make the transition called death. Then, at the time of death, we shed this cocoon and are once again as free as a butterfly to use the symbolic language that we use when talking to dying children and their siblings. . . .

Being a skeptical semi-believer, to put it mildly, and not interested in issues of life after death, I could not help but be impressed by several observations which occurred so frequently that I began to wonder why nobody ever studied the real issues of death. Not for any special scientific reasons, not to cover lawsuits, needless to say, but simply out of natural curiosity.

Man has existed for forty-seven million years and has been in its present existence, which includes the facet of divinity, for seven million years. Every day people die all over the world. Yet in a society that is able to send a man to the moon and bring him back well and safe, we have never put any effort into the definition of human death. Isn't that peculiar?

So in the midst of caring for dying patients and the teaching of medical and seminary students, we decided one day on the spur of the moment that we would try to come up with a new, updated, all-inclusive definition of death. It is said somewhere: "Ask and you will be given, knock and the door will be opened." Or in another way: "A teacher will appear when the student is ready.". . .

Sudden Death Experiences

We can say, after all these years of collecting data, that the following points are common denominators in all those cases of people who have had a near-death experience. Also relevant is the fact that they had these experiences after an accident, murder attempt, suicide attempt, or a slow lingering death. Over half of our cases have been sudden death experiences, therefore the patients would have not been able to prepare or anticipate an experience. At the moment of death, all of you will experience the separation of the real immortal

You, from the temporary house, namely the physical body. We will call this immortal self the soul or the entity, or using the symbolic language that we use when we communicate with children, we call it the butterfly in the process of leaving the cocoon. When we leave the physical body there will be a total absence of panic, fear, or anxiety. We will always experience a physical wholeness and will be totally aware of the environment in which this accident or death occurs. This may be a hospital room, our own bedroom after experiencing a coronary attack at home, or after a tragic car accident or a plane crash. We will be quite aware of the people who work with the resuscitation team, or the people who work in a rescue attempt to extricate a mutilated and hurt body from a car wreck. We will watch this at the distance of a few feet, in a rather detached state of mind, if I may use the word mind, though we are no longer connected with the mind or functioning brain at this moment in most cases.

This all occurs at the time when we have no measurable signs of brain activity. It happens very often at the time when physicians find no signs of life whatsoever. At this moment of observation of the scene of death we will be aware of people's conversation, their behavior, their attire, and their thoughts without having any negative feelings about the whole occurrence.

Our second body, which we experience at this time, is not the physical body but an ethereal body. . . . In the second, temporary, ethereal body we experience a total wholeness as I said before. If we have been amputees, we will have our legs again. If we have been deaf mutes, we can hear and talk and sing. If we have been a multiple-sclerosis patient in a wheelchair with blurred vision, blurred speech, and unable to move our legs, we are able to sing and dance again.

It is understandable that many of our patients who have been successfully resuscitated are not always grateful when their butterfly is squashed back into the cocoon, since with the revival of our bodily functions we also have to accept the pains and the handicaps that go with it. In the state of the ethereal body, we have no pain and no handicaps.

Many of my colleagues wondered if this is not simply projection of our wishful thinking, which could be very understandable and comprehensible. If anyone has been paralyzed, mute, blind, or handicapped for many, many years, they may be looking forward to a time when their suffering is ended.

It is very easy to evaluate whether this is a projection of wishful thinking or not. Half of our cases have been sudden, unexpected accidents or near-death experiences where people who were unable to foresee what was going to hit them, as in the case of a hit-and-run driver who amputated the legs of one of our patients. When the patient was out of his physical body, he saw his amputated legs on a highway, yet he was fully aware of having both of his legs on his ethereal, perfect, and whole body. We cannot assume that he had previous knowledge of the loss of his legs and would therefore project in his own wishful thinking that he would be able to walk again.

But there is a much simpler way to rule out the projection of wishful thinking, and that is to study blind people who do not have light perception. We asked them to share with us what it was like when they had this near-death experience. If it was just wish fulfillment, these blind people would not be able to share with us the color of a sweater, the design of a tie, or many details of shape, colors, and designs of people's clothing. We have questioned several totally blind people and they were not only able to tell us who came into the room first and who worked on the resuscitation, but they were able to give minute details of the attire and the clothing of all the people present, something a totally blind person would never be able to do.

Reincarnation Is Evidence of Life After Death

Philip Kapleau

Most Eastern religions believe in reincarnation, or the belief that a person's soul never dies. After the death of the body, the soul travels to a new host. Reincarnation is gaining popularity, even in Christian religions. Many believe the Bible makes references to reincarnation. It is also becoming more and more acceptable to combine traditional Judeo-Christian beliefs with Eastern beliefs. Today, many Americans are devoted followers of Eastern religions.

Zenmaster Philip Kapleau introduced Zen to America during the 1960s. As a follower of Japanese Buddhism, Kapleau is considered an expert in matters of reincarnation. The following was taken from a seminar Kapleau held and later included in his book *The Wheel of Life and Death*. It answers many questions about reincarnation and explains why Kapleau believes that reincarnation proves there is life after death.

Philip Kapleau, *The Wheel of Life and Death: A Practical and Spiritual Guide.* New York: Doubleday, 1989. Copyright © 1989 by The Zen Center, a New York not-for-profit religious corporation. Reproduced by permission.

"As far back as I can remember I have unconsciously referred to the experiences of a previous state of existence. . . . As the stars looked to me when I was a shepherd in Assyria, they look to me now a New Englander. . . . And Hawthorne, too, I remember as one with whom I sauntered in old heroic times along the banks of the Scamander amid the ruins of chariots and heroes."

Perhaps you've heard or read statements such as this before and dismissed them as no more than the fantasies of a starry-eyed New Ager or an Eastern guru. Surely no one with both feet on the ground could believe that he had lived in other bodies in times past, and that he even remembered those lives. Yet these are not the ravings of a lunatic or the pseudophilosophic musings of someone strung out on drugs. These are the words of Henry David Thoreau—a man of lively mind, to be sure, but as American as apple pie.

The Intermediate Realm

It is the teaching of sages from Buddhist and other cultures that at the moment of death we begin our transitional existence, which is the intermediate realm between death and rebirth. This realm is very different from the physical plane, but in one respect it is identical. For just as our ego-based perceptions affect the way we relate to and interact with our environment and events in this world, similarly does our karma, stemming from both the last and many former existences, affect the way we relate to the experiences of an intermediate life.

There are said to be three primary stages in the transitional state. The initial stage consists predominantly of physical sensations of freedom and is relatively short in duration. At this point a tenuous connection to the physical body still remains. One may be acutely aware of the actions and words as well as the thoughts of living loved ones. This sensitivity and awareness mean that any words *directed to the deceased* at this time—as in chanting, for example—can bring about an awakening.

The second stage encompasses diverse sensory experiences and lasts longer than the first. In the final stage the entity is drawn, according to its karma, to a particular rebirth. The process from death to rebirth is said to take place in cycles of seven days or multiples thereof—usually forty-nine days. But this figure is not fixed. It can occur in a day or a week or not until many years later. Presumably the time of rebirth is determined by, among other factors, the attraction of the being to parents with whom it has a karmic affinity.

PSYCHOLOGIST: *How is it possible to know about such things as this? You're talking about what happens after someone is dead.*

Some extremely psychic people have the capacity to recall all the stages of death leading from one life to the next. There is also the testimony of some of the ancient masters in the Tibetan *Book of the Dead,* a text which traces a person's journey from dying to rebirth and teaches the art of dying peacefully in order to obtain a propitious rebirth. This book leads one, in vivid detail, through the various stages of that journey. Valuable as it is, it has the disadvantage of being written in language too quaint or esoteric for modern readers.

NURSE: *Since some people are able to remember these things, there must be some sort of sensory consciousness that remains after death.*

As I mentioned earlier, the seventh, eighth, and ninth levels of consciousness do survive death. Or you could say karma, or the force of will, continues in its cyclic propulsion through death, after-death, and rebirth. But we also possess a semblance of our other senses in the intermediate existence. At the moment of death the first six levels of consciousness become transmuted from a physical orientation to a nonphysical. Until we take on a "solid" body again, sight, hearing, smell, taste, touch, and intellect are incipient, functioning in a tenuous way. Without a body as a vehicle they cannot be fully utilized, but neither are they completely absent. . . .

Understanding the Next Realm

DANCE INSTRUCTOR: Can you tell us in more detail about this realm?

It is as difficult to give a precise description of the *intermediate state* as it is to give one of this world—only more so. Since, as I've said, the experience of passage is colored by our karma, it will differ from person to person. However, it is possible to give what might be called an Everyman's (or -woman's) description of this state.

Let me capitulate in some detail the masters' accounts of the stages of the journey from death to rebirth. During the first stage the most striking element is the thought of how easy it is to die. Unlike the sometimes prolonged act of dying, which may be difficult and painful, death itself is as simple, easy, and natural as a leaf's fluttering off a tree. Many people see their whole life played out rapidly before them in the instant before physical death. Soon after that, as the intermediate state of existence is entered, there may be a feeling of floating or flying, similar to sensations people often have in dreams. There is an awareness of great calmness and tranquillity, a sensation of relief and utter ease. One might even wonder, "What was all the worry about?" With the last breath all worries and cares of the mundane world are cast aside. The entity may then be drawn to a tunnel of bright white light and may sense that loved ones or a wonderful experience lies in wait at the end. The feeling is like that of walking into a lover's embrace, or like the joyful anticipation of a child waiting to open presents on Christmas morning.

The events and experiences of this first stage are substantially the same whether a person has very negative, pain-producing karma or relatively good karma. However, the way a person with bad karma relates to these experiences will be considerably different from the way a person with good karma does. The former might, for example, feel cynical, suffused with apprehension and suspicion. At first such a person may feel that he "got away with it," that is, with the crimes and evil perpetrated in his life, but he will soon become uneasy. What is happening will be perceived as a loss of control, and his anxiety will grow.

The second stage of passage is deeply influenced by a person's mind state at the time of death. Also of great importance are the life experiences of the being both in its last previous lifetime and in its many former lifetimes, as well as the kind of guidance received in the immediate post-death state. Here again, is where strong, meaningful chanting at the funeral can be effective. Thus the experience of the second stage varies extensively from person to person. The experiences encountered, however, are all projections of one's own consciousness, and if this is understood and firmly imbedded in the mind, one will not be frightened by the apparitions that may appear.

HOMEMAKER: *Since the first stage of dying is so pleasant, why can't a person who wishes strongly enough just remain there?*

Because merely having the desire is not enough. More important is great spiritual strength. . . .

For most people, then, it is inevitable that they enter the second stage. When it begins, the intermediate entity may feel confused, as if awakening from a deep, drugged sleep. Everything will seem vaguely familiar and dreamlike, as though the being were caught in a constant state of déjà vu.

Many different things may happen now. The senses, which were once accustomed to the simple and mundane things of the physical world, will be assaulted by various frightening, terrible, or exquisitely beautiful sights, sounds, and smells. Loud, startling noises, sudden bangs, cracks, and rumbles will be heard. Howling wind and raging fires may appear. The entity may feel as if it is sinking into an abyss or becoming paralyzed. Words are spoken, but no sound is heard; sounds are heard, but no words are spoken. Thoughts wander randomly, as in a delirium. It is not possible to focus on objects, because they move away or become transparent. Nothing appears solid, nothing has substance. It is possible to move like a flash of lightning, at great speeds through objects. All of the senses, though of a tenuous nature, are present, but they are no longer attuned to the physical realm.

A Child's Karma

HOMEMAKER: *Would even a young child or an infant experience these frightening things?*

It depends entirely on its karma. Remember, after death there is no such thing as age or even sex. In this sense, death is the great equalizer. What *does* remain, though, are the conditioning karmic seeds that were planted throughout many life times. Also of extreme importance is one's last thought at the time of death. If a child died peacefully—say, in her sleep or in her mother's arms—the chances are her last thought would be a positive one. If, on the other hand, she died violently, her last thought would very likely be filled with fear, confusion, hatred, or other turbulent emotions. It is a mistake to think of a child as "only" a child. In one sense, of course, he is only as old as his physical body, but in another, a child is as ageless as the universe—as we all are. A person's physical form, looked at from birth to death, is no more than a temporary stopping point, a momentary embodiment. One should not be misled by it. An infant of two months, a man of seventy years—at death there is no difference between them other than their self-created karmic load.

It is vital to understand that the way an individual reacts to the transitional experiences greatly depends on the kind of life he led before dying. Whether he is frightened by these experiences or unmoved by them depends on the degree to which he saw through his clinging attachments to the material world. And his reactions to events now will determine much of what is yet to come.

The masters have assured us that everything one experiences in this state is as unreal and devoid of substance, as empty of all abiding reality, as what is experienced in the dimension of waking consciousness. All lights, visions, and apparitions of every kind should therefore be regarded as mere projections and reflexes of the entity's mind states. Since the terrifying things it encounters cannot cause harm, it need not cower before them. The being should now remind itself of the need to be free from all clinging attachments to objects as well as experiences. If the entity was experienced in meditation during former existences and developed concentrative powers to a high degree, it will still have the ability to focus its mind. It is possible to accomplish this if there is single-minded concentration on the truths one has understood. Although the entity may feel as if it is in the midst of a raging storm, it can become tranquil and centered through the concentrative power of its mind.

When the second stage draws to an end, the third stage begins. As with the first two stages, here too karma plays an all-important role. This is the time when one, so to speak, looks into the mirror of her karma and finds herself committed to a particular course of action. According to the causes and conditions established, the entity will be drawn to one of a number of realms in which rebirth will take place. Those who have led destructive, pain-producing lives will be inexorably drawn to a rebirth that will entail great suffering. Those who have led more wholesome lives will also be drawn toward rebirths that are in accord with their deeds.

It should be emphasized that the impulse to be reborn is devoid of all self-conscious reflection or cognition. It is rather a blind yearning toward the mother-to-be on the part of one who will be reborn as a male, or toward the father-to-be for one who will be reborn as a female. This instinct is governed by our karma, which induces us to be attracted to a particular type of environmental and physical existence— well-to-do or humble, male or female, human or nonhuman, dark- or fair-skinned, Chinese, Mexican, African, or American. The body can thus be described as a crystallization of thought patterns conditioned by our karma—a process that began before birth and that will continue after it in an infinite expansion of life.

We can rightly say that we contain the seeds of past memories and the vestiges of recollections of former lives, not excluding the former lives of others. The scholar John Blofeld describes this well:

> What we call "life" is a single link in an infinitely long chain of "lives" and "deaths." Perhaps, if our unconscious could be raised to conscious level, we should be able to perceive the entire chain stretching back far enough to exceed the most generous estimates of the length of time human beings have populated this earth. (And why just this earth? Why should not many of our previous lives have been passed upon other earths contained within this stupendous universe?) Perhaps the recollection would include hundreds or thousands of millions of lives lived here or elsewhere, and at this or other levels of consciousness, perhaps in states of being previously unsuspected.

Contemporary Belief in Reincarnation

. . . In our own time, too, we persist in refusing to accept death as the incontrovertible end. According to a Gallup poll taken in 1980–81, nearly 70 percent of Americans believe in life after death. While most people's concept of an afterlife is based on a union with God, reunion with loved ones, and/or life in a heavenly realm, a surprising 23 percent believe in reincarnation. What is surprising is not that such a great number believe in the continuity of existence, but rather that so *few* Americans embrace what is, for a large proportion of the world's population—Hindus, Buddhists, and Jains, as well as others—incontrovertible.

Many outstanding individuals of our age—Carl Jung, Ralph Waldo Emerson, Albert Schweitzer, Henry David Thoreau, and Mohandas Gandhi, to name just a few—believed in reincarnation, transmigration, or rebirth. . . . Belief in reincarnation, if not rebirth, is not inimical to contemporary Christian and Jewish beliefs. Dr. Leslie Weatherhead, minister of London's City Temple for almost three decades, felt that reincarnation offered a key to unlock many problems for Christians. He pointed out that Jesus never denied it, that it was a prevailing belief in Jesus' day, and that it was an essential part of the Essene teachings.

Passages in the Old Testament and the Kabala, sacred texts of Judaism, contain references to metempsychosis, or transmigration. It is also universally accepted by the Hasidic movement. Commenting on the origins of Jewish belief in transmigration, Rabbi Moses Gaster says, "There cannot be any doubt that these views are extremely old [in Judaism]. Simon Magus raises the claim of former existences, his soul passing through many bodies before it reaches that known as Simon. . . . The [Hebrew] masters of the occult science never doubted its Jewish character. . . ."

To the ordinary modern Westerner, however, rebirth,

which is commonly misunderstood to be synonymous with reincarnation, is perceived as no more than a superstitious fantasy, something to be relegated to the domain of the channeler, spiritualist, and New Ager. Few prominent people in the sciences or the humanities will say forthrightly, as did Dean William Inge, "I find it both credible and attractive."

Is Rebirth the Goal of Life?

PSYCHOTHERAPIST: *Why bother living if the only goal of life is to die so that you can start over again with a clean slate?*

Rebirth is *not* the goal. The ultimate "goal," to use this imprecise term, of a person with an aspiration to awakening is not rebirth—and with it the inevitable pains and sufferings attendant upon a body—but the unconditioned state of pure consciousness. What the true aspirant seeks is release from the pain and frustrations of numberless lives, from the endless wheel of rebirths, both for himself and for all beings. . . .

Simply stated, what propels us again and again into rebirth is the desire, the craving, the will for another body, coupled with the tightly held notion of oneself as a discrete entity. Rebirth, then, is the inevitable consequence of our not having attained full awakening and total integration in this lifetime. At the same time rebirth is another opportunity for awakening, assuming of course that one incarnates as a human being again. Remember, it is only through a human body that we can come to enlightenment—this is why human life is so precious. "Reexistence," then, is a halfway house on the way to one's true home. As Gandhi said (speaking of attaining the goal of *ahimsā* or nonviolence), "I cannot think of permanent enmity between man and man, and believing as I do in the theory of rebirth, I live in the hope that if not in this birth, in some other birth I shall be able to hug all humanity in friendly embrace."

Rebirth Distinguished from Reincarnation

DANCE INSTRUCTOR: I am confused about the difference between reincarnation, which I take to be the transmigration of souls, and rebirth. You said they were not the same.

The doctrines of transmigration and reincarnation imply the existence of a soul and are simplifications of the teaching of rebirth, which is, admittedly, more difficult to grasp. The problem lies in the key term "soul." What we call our soul, or our self, is actually no more than a current of consciousness comprised of "thought-moments of infinitesimal duration succeeding one another in a stream of inconceivable rapidity." The speed and progress of this process, although always of lightning-fast duration, change according to the nature of the stimulation. If the catalyst is slight, the process functions without full cognition.

We can compare the process to a movie: the illusion of motion is created by numerous still frames moving in swift progression. It is also like a river: the body of water rushing before us is in reality made up of innumerable droplets of water flowing together.

DANCE INSTRUCTOR: Doesn't what you are talking about differ from what we think of as soul?

The Buddhist scholar Francis Story explains "soul" more precisely:

> Much misunderstanding of the Buddhist doctrine of rebirth has been caused in the West by the use of the words "reincarnation," "transmigration" and "soul.". . ."Soul" is an ambiguous term that has never been clearly defined in Western religious thought; but it is generally taken to mean the sum total of an individual personality, an enduring ego-entity that exists more or less independently of the physical body and survives it after death. The "soul" is considered to be the personality-factor which distinguishes one individual from another, and is supposed to consist of the elements of consciousness, mind, character and all that goes to make up the

psychic, immaterial side of a human being.

The Buddha categorically denied the existence of a "soul" in the sense defined above. He recognized that all conditioned and compounded phenomena are impermanent, and this alone makes the existence of such a "soul" impossible.

Reincarnation implies an independent, migrating soul substance that embodies itself in a new form. The teaching of rebirth, or the continuity of life, repudiates such a notion. . . .

What Is Reborn?

NURSE: Just what is *it, then, that is reborn?*

To give it a name is to twist the truth to suit ourselves. An enlightened master said simply, "Not he, yet not another." Buddhaghosa, another sage, said, "It is a mere material and immaterial state, arising when it has obtained its conditions . . . it is not a lasting being, not a soul.". . .

Intuition Versus Scientific Proof

DANCE INSTRUCTOR: It seems to me that much of what you theologians are saying relies on intuition. There's nothing wrong with that, of course, but you seem to imply that scientists should be willing to accept on pure faith what you have learned through intuition. But intuition can never be proved.

True, intuition, which is the faculty of immediate and direct cognition, is not amenable to proof by the methods of science; yet it is inherent in all of us and needs only to be developed. As Emerson points out, the sacred books of each nation are the sanctuary of the intuitions. Since intuition is the means by which we fathom transcendental religious truths, it should be respected as another mode of cognition. As an aspect of the mystical, it cannot be conceptually grasped. Science, too, partakes of the mystical. [Albert] Einstein and other outstanding men of science have said that their greatest discoveries came, not through logical thinking, but through an intuitive leap.

Science deals with the time-space dimension, with the world apprehended by the senses and the intellect; religion deals with the *scientist*, with his longing for self-transcendence and Self-fulfillment. The spiritually awakened know that the phenomenal world, the province of science, is only one half—or more properly, one aspect—of reality and that inner peace, more certainty, and true wisdom come when this world of forms has been transcended *but not abandoned.*

Science and religion need not be rivals; they can be mutually reinforcing. Science without a spiritual outlook is barren and socially dangerous. Religion bolstered by science is better able to keep its feet on the ground while its head is in the heavens. Dr. Robert Jastrow, himself a highly respected scientist, affirms in vivid language the central role of religion: "For the scientist who has lived by his faith in the power of reason, the story ends like a bad dream. He has scaled the mountains of ignorance; he is about to conquer the highest peak. As he pulls himself over the final rock, he is greeted by a band of theologians who have been sitting there for centuries."

Also be aware that as regards proof, there is a fundamental difference in philosophic outlook between the cultures of the East and the West. The attitude of Western philosophy is that "what is *not proved* is to be treated as false." The attitude of Eastern philosophy is that "what is *not proved* may be accepted as true until *proved* to be false," particularly if supported by our intuition, experience, and/or reason.

The Power of Will

PSYCHOLOGIST: *You mentioned in passing that the force that continues after death can be designated the power of will. Could you explain this further?*

The power of will is a tremendous force to be reckoned

with. Anyone who has had a two-year-old can attest to that. This will has the power to extend through lifetimes.

A parable illustrating this principle goes like this: A man was determined to empty all the water from a vast lake in order to find a priceless pearl lying at the bottom. After two or three days of the man's emptying bucket after bucket of water, a huge dragon appeared and said to him, "I am the lord of this lake. What are you doing?" The man answered that he was searching for the lost pearl and that he intended to empty every drop of water from the lake until he found it.

The dragon laughed at him and said derisively, "You will never find it. It is impossible for you to empty all the water, even were you to do nothing else for your entire life." But the man kept on emptying bucket after bucket. "You are wrong," he said. "I will succeed. For even if I don't empty the lake in this life, I will die with nothing else on my mind than to get the jewel. In my next lifetime I will return to the lake and continue my work. When I die, I will again be reborn and will again persist. Even if it takes me one hundred, one thousand, ten thousand lifetimes, eventually I will succeed and the pearl will be mine." The dragon, struck by the man's fierce determination, realized that nothing could stop him and that he (the dragon) would eventually lose not only the jewel but his lake as well, so he gave the pearl to the man.

Swami Vivekananda (1863–1902) wrote vividly of the will that perseveres through successive births:

> Such a gigantic will as that of a Buddha or Jesus could not be obtained in one life, for we know who their fathers were. It is not known that their fathers ever spoke a word for the good of mankind. The gigantic will which manifested Buddha and Jesus—whence came this accumulation of power? It must have been there through ages and ages, continually growing bigger and bigger until it burst on society as Buddha or Jesus, and it is rolling down even to the present day.

Of all the needs we have—to create, to know, to experience life—nothing can compare with the will to develop oneself spiritually in order to free oneself and others from suffering. Yet it takes countless *lifetimes* of dedicated effort and single-minded determination in order to develop one's potential to the fullest so that this can be accomplished. It is impossible to burst full-blown into the world as a completely enlightened person without such preparation. Since the will to live again is conditioned by a need for self-development, a person will very likely be drawn to the state of existence most conducive to that activity. Remember: it is the *desire* or craving for a continuation of life, and the clinging to a notion of a separate individuality, that propel us again and again into new rounds of birth and death. This is why, when the Buddhist sage Nāgasena was asked by King Milinda whether or not he would be reborn after death, Nāgasena replied, "If when I die I die with craving for existence in my heart, yes; but if not, no."

Rebirth Is Not Always a Step Up

SOCIOLOGIST: *Well, if we've been reborn so many times, how come we're not better people? Why do we still kill and maim and generally ruin this planet we live on?*

Don't forget that a person's succeeding life isn't always a step up. If that person has set up negative causes and conditions in the past, they will ripen eventually, and that could mean a drop to a much lower rung on the ladder of existence. Given most people's limited vision, it is extremely difficult and painful to continue to do the things one needs to do to develop into a fully grown human being. A person who has truly seen into his True-nature—and this is possible for each one of us—has the advantage of knowing what he or she has to do. This is often accompanied with the strength—developed through steady and regular practice of meditation—to transcend the pain and difficulties that may accompany self-development.

The Will to Live Makes Man Re-Live

DANCE INSTRUCTOR: Do we actually have the power to choose the type of existence into which we will be reborn? It almost sounds as if you are saying that you'd better watch out, because you'll probably get what you want.

That's not far from the truth. Remember the song that went something like "You can't always get what you want. . . . But you might find you get what you need"? Well, that's closer to it. What we *think* we want is often just a reflection of our superficial desires. Our deepest yearnings push and pull us on a subconscious level and drive us to what we truly need—even if it's not what we *think* we need or want. [Writer] Oscar Wilde expressed this perfectly when he said that there are two kinds of unhappiness in the world: not getting what you want, and getting what you want.

There is another element also at work here. We could call it the principle of "like attracts like." The subconscious mind exerts a tremendous power to draw to itself others of similar inclination. People feel most comfortable with those who share similar interests and values: artists enjoy hobnobbing with other artists, musicians enjoy the company of musically inclined people, and the spiritually minded will commune with those who share their interests. On the other hand, thieves associate with underworld characters, drinkers with alcoholics, drug addicts with pushers; neurotics seek the company of other neurotics, and the mentally disturbed gravitate toward people who are unbalanced. On both a conscious and subconscious level we create our environment even as we participate in it.

So long as there is *desire* for rebirth, repeated rebirths will take place in various existences. Indeed, attachment itself, the craving, brings about the next birth. V.F. Gunaratna puts it epigrammatically: "The will-to-live makes man re-live."

SOCIOLOGIST: If all it takes to be reborn again and again is to want to be reborn, you'd think that this fact would relieve the anxieties of a lot of people who think death means extinction— the end.

Oddly, in our culture not too many people believe that it is possible. But a belief in rebirth *would* relieve one's anxiety about dying if one felt that in his life he had not created unwholesome karma. The hitch is that one's next existence will be on a lower or higher level, depending on the kind of life one has lived—whether a pain-producing one or a more or less selfless life. An employer, say, who was the epitome of greed, exploiting his employees and others mercilessly, might find himself in a hellish existence in his next life, suffering retribution for his inhumane behavior.

On the other hand, if you are able to die free of the fear of dying and without the conscious or unconscious wish to be reborn—merely asking yourself in the words of an ancient Zen master (Bassui), "What is the true essence of the Mind of this one who is now suffering [dying]"—you will eventually be freed of your painful bondage to endless change.

SOCIOLOGIST: So what happens to such an individual?

I don't know. I suppose the ancients would call him a divine immortal. For most living beings, though, the attachment to life is so strong that escaping from the pull of endless rounds of birth and death is immensely difficult. While still a bodhisattva [one who refrains from entering nirvana in order to save others] Gautama (the Buddha-to-be) is said to have been reborn into animal and human realms some 550 times before attaining full Buddhahood.

HOMEMAKER: Suppose a person doesn't want to be reborn because she is frightened of the results of negative things she did throughout her life.

A deeply spiritual person is not frightened of being reborn, because she understands the root cause of birth and death and calmly accepts the consequences of her actions, be they good or bad. It is only because such a person is without fear that she can die free from thoughts of body or not-body. Then, too, a highly developed person might willingly be reborn, taking on a body out of love—love and compassion for those who are still suffering and who need help to come to true understanding.

Your question brings up another important point. It is impossible to live a life full of fear, anger, and pain-producing actions and then, at the moment of death, escape from karmic retribution by having a "good" thought. Although a person might be afraid of rebirth and try to suppress the desire for another body, it is not possible to do so, because the habit forces of many lifetimes are still operating at the moment of death. The last thought of a dying person has an initial impact on the rebirth, but the cumulative effect of the events of his or her life exerts a tremendous additional influence. With respect to the person you mentioned, her next rebirth would be conditioned by her fear of retribution in that life. Accordingly, she might be reborn agoraphobic or severely repressed, or as a withdrawn, timid individual afraid of her own shadow. But in any case, she certainly would be reborn. Fear is a clinging to that which we fear; perversely, it is this clinging that brings us the very thing we fear or would most like to avoid.

PSYCHOLOGIST: *Are you implying that a person can come into life with fears already established?*

Yes. There are many cases of people who have severe, unexplained fears that have been present from their earliest childhood. Children sometimes have aversions that border on the hysterical. I remember one mother telling me about her child. She said that he had been petrified of large bodies of water from the time he was an infant. He would be fine in the bathtub, but if they went on an outing to the beach, he screamed in such terror that they had to leave. He is a teenager now and he still does not enjoy being around lakes or oceans, although he is no longer as visibly frightened.

How would you explain such a phenomenon? If you look at the problem from the point of view of rebirth, it is entirely possible that the young man died at sea in a previous lifetime and took with him into his current life a terror connected with the experience. Naturally, there can be other interpretations for such fears, but this one is seldom, if ever, considered by traditional psychoanalysts.

Nonetheless, a number of therapists do concur in the belief that many of our fears and neuroses actually stem from causes in prior existences. Such people, who call themselves past-life therapists, hypnotically regress their patients into one or more previous lifetimes to search for the trauma that is creating a problem for them in this life.

A Religious View of Life After Death

Leighton Ford

Perhaps the most common belief in life after death is the Christian belief that when a person dies they pass on to either heaven or hell. According to the Bible, there is an afterlife. If people are saved, they go to heaven; if they are not, they go to hell. Daniel 12:2 states, "Many . . . shall awake, some to everlasting life, and some to shame and everlasting contempt."

Leighton Ford, a minister and the president of Leighton Ford Ministries, has spent his life communicating the word of God to people all over the world. The following excerpt is from a sermon delivered by Ford. In his sermon, Ford explains why he believes heaven is a fact, what heaven is like, and even how to get to heaven.

W hat is heaven? What do we know about it? First of all, we know from what the Bible tells us that heaven is a place.

Leighton Ford, "Hope for a Great Forever," www.PreachingTodaySermons.com, a resource of Christianity Today International. Copyright © by Leighton Ford. Reproduced by permission.

Jesus said, "In my Father's house are many rooms; if it were not so, I would have told you. I am going there to prepare a place for you.". . . When Jesus said this, he was gathered with his disciples. In a few hours their world was going to cave in. The sun was going to come down at midnight. The Lord they loved was going to be taken from them, and Jesus said to them, "Don't let your hearts be troubled. Trust in God." Sometimes we have to accept and trust when we can't understand. Jesus went on to say, "Trust also in me. In my father's house are many rooms. . . . I am going there to prepare a place for you."

Heaven is a real place. That doesn't mean heaven is up in the sense that we say, "Well, heaven is up beyond the stars some place." Heaven isn't a place that you can see with a telescope, if you had one strong enough. Heaven isn't a place where you could arrive on a space ship even if you had one that could fly far enough. Heaven is not contained in time and in space. It's another realm of existence and another dimension entirely.

You might wonder why I believe in heaven in an age like this. One of the Russian cosmonauts came back and said, "Some people say God lives out there. I looked around, and I didn't see any God out there." [Reverend] Billy Graham's wife, Ruth, says he looked in the wrong place. If he'd stepped outside the space ship without his space suit, he would have seen God very quickly.

In this age we wonder if we should believe in that any more. We hear stories of people who seem to die for a short time and are resuscitated. When they come back, they say, "I saw a great figure of light out there." Other people say they go through a tunnel, and then see this being of light. Jerry Lewis, the comedian, said, "I was on the other side not long ago when my heart stopped. It was like a television screen where the picture goes down, and there's a point, and then there's nothing." Other people say, "I saw an image of hell, and it scared me."

Four Reasons to Believe in Heaven

What are we to believe? I believe in heaven for four reasons. First because Jesus taught it. Jesus said, "I go to prepare a place for you." And notice what he said. "If it were not so, would I have told you that I go to prepare a place?" Jesus says, "You can believe me."

And all Christians believe in the word of Jesus Christ. Jesus said, "If it were not so, I wouldn't fool you. I wouldn't give you an illusion, which is not true. If it were not true, I would have told you." Evangelist David Livingston said this about Jesus' word, "It's the word of a perfect gentleman. He never lies." I say it's more than that. It's also the Word of God. Jesus taught it.

I believe in heaven also because our hearts call for it. Our hearts long for it because there's something within our human experience that cannot be satisfied with anything on this earth. After King Solomon had tried pleasure, money, entertainment, wisdom, and culture, he said "I tried it all, and it was vanity." Then he said, "God has put eternity in our hearts."

Have you tried the waters of earth? You've run after them and they've trickled away. You've tried pleasure, money, and success, maybe even the good pleasures of this life. If you're honest with yourself tonight, you know they haven't satisfied. We long for more.

I read about two teenagers in Chicago who wanted to prove their love for each other. They went to the top of a six story building, kissed each other, and jumped off. They left a note saying, "We're looking for a better place." The girl was killed. The boy was seriously injured. I thought, I wish someone had told them there is a better place. Earth is a better place when Christ comes and lives within. Heaven is a better place. You don't have to jump off the roof of a building.

[Fyodor] Dostoyevsky, the great Russian novelist said, "Surely I haven't suffered simply that I may manure the soil of the future for someone else.". . .

I also believe in heaven because science by no means rules it out. Somehow we have the idea that our generation has learned so much scientifically that it has exploded the idea of heaven and God. I remember talking to the director of the space laboratory in Huntsville, Alabama, where we held a crusade. He said, "Dr. Ford, the more I learn about space, the greater my understanding of God is."

Dr. Irwin Moon of the Moody Institute of Science was talking to a very famous scientist who said to him, "Dr. Moon, I don't understand how you as an intelligent scientist can say you believe in heaven. According to the Bible, the first man to die was Abel when Cain killed him. If Abel had traveled at the speed of light for six thousand years he wouldn't have reached the edge of the universe, which we can see with our telescope. He'd have thousands of years to go before he could get to heaven."

Dr. Moon replied, "Am I not correct? Are you not the scientist who has put forward the notion that matter is really porous and that it's possible to have a solid wall which really is mostly space?" The scientist said, "Of course that's true. I believe that."

Then Dr. Moon said, "Would it not be possible to have two different worlds occupying the same space provided they were synchronized so they were on different frequencies?" After a moment, the scientist said, "Of course it would. You could have thousands of worlds." Then Dr. Moon said, "Sir, to go to heaven, I may not have to move an inch. All I'll have to do is change frequencies."

Most of all, I believe in heaven because the resurrection

of Jesus Christ confirms it. Jesus said, "Because I live, you shall live also." Jesus' disciples said they saw him crucified, but God raised him. They said, "We ate with him after the resurrection. We drank with him. We talked with him. We saw him. We had breakfast by the lake with him. We touched him. He was alive again."

He was the same Jesus, and yet they said he was different. He could suddenly appear in a locked room, then suddenly he was gone. They would see him, and then they wouldn't see him. He was the same, and yet he was different. In I Corinthians 15 Paul says those who are in Christ bear the image of the earthly and will bear the image of the heavenly. We are to have a new form—a new body. You put seeds into the ground in one form, and they come up in the beautiful form of these flowers. It's identical, and it's different.

Heaven Is Our Eternal Address

In Christ we are going to have a new body for that new home where we're going. Yes, heaven is a place. Heaven is your eternal address. I want to say to every person here tonight: you may have lost your way, and some of you have, but don't lose your address. Concerned with the things of earth, you've forgotten the things of God. Maybe at some point you disobeyed and sinned and wandered off. Maybe in the acids of modern skepticism, you've lost your way. Don't lose your address, Friend. Your address is in the heart of God. Don't deny that hunger in your soul. Don't say, "This is all I need in this earth." Don't say heaven isn't there. Homesickness is a gift from God to remind us we are all pilgrims and strangers. Even though we live in one of the most beautiful parts of the world, this is a temporary place. Yes, heaven is a place. God is saying tonight, "Come home. Come home where you belong.". . .

Heaven is also a prepared place. Jesus said, "I go to prepare a place for you." In the Bible Jesus is called the fore-runner. That's like the advance party in the army. Some of you men out here were probably scouts in the army. You'd go ahead of the rest of the troops to see that the way was safe and to blaze a trail. Jesus was the scout. He's the advance party, the forerunner. He says, "I've gone to open the way into heaven and into the presence of God. I've gone to prepare a place for you.". . .

What Is Heaven Like?

What's heaven like? I've heard some people say, "I don't think I want to go to heaven. I think it's going to be very boring up there, all these bald business men playing harps forever." What's it like? 1 Corinthians 2:9 says, "No eye has seen, no ear has heard, no mind has conceived what God has prepared for those who love him."

I don't think we can understand very much about heaven yet because we're so space-bound, so time-bound. Our activities in this world are so self-centered. In heaven there is no time; there are no limitations of space; everything is centered around God. To talk about heaven is like telling pygmies in a rain forest in Africa about a space trip. It's difficult for us to understand. Scripture says we cannot comprehend it, but God has revealed it to us by his Spirit.

What has God revealed to us about heaven? First, he's told us what will not be there. Revelation 21:4: "There will be no more death or mourning or crying or pain, for the old order of things has passed away." All of those things that bring misery here—grief, hurt, sickness, death—will be gone.

Second, he's told us what will be there. Love will be there. Love never fails. Heaven will be a community of love. People will be there—those who have been redeemed. In many ways we will be the same but different—just as Jesus was different and yet the same Jesus. We'll recognize and know each other and take much of our uniqueness into that new life.

Third, heaven will be a place of dynamic activity. We're not going to sit around twiddling our thumbs on a cloud forever. The Scripture says in heaven we will serve God. Revelation 22:3: "And his servants will serve him." We're going to rest from sin in heaven but not from service.

When our son Sandy died at the age of 21, a missionary who had overseen his work as a summer missionary in France wrote us a letter, and he said, "I was stunned—21. So many gifts to use. I thought, What a waste." Then he said, "Leighton, I realize we are so earthbound. Sandy's highest service has only begun."

Nothing is wasted because God will have ways for us to serve him. I don't know what that might be. I don't know how that works, but the Bible does say we will serve him.

It says we will see God. His servants will see him. We shall see him as he is. Far from being boring, can you imagine how your mind will expand with the vision of the greatness of God? Talk about intellectual stimulation. There's nothing you've ever studied that will be like that.

Life After Death Theories Are Provable

Victor Zammit

Paranormal activity, quantum physics, and mystical occurrences are common examples of unusual happenings often debunked by critics. There are many publications and organizations such as the Committee for the Scientific Investigation of Claims of the Paranormal, or CSICOP, that are devoted to finding fallacy in claims made by researchers of paranormal activity. Victor Zammit has been on both sides. As a researcher and explorer of the paranormal, he discovered that critics were often too rigid and narrow-minded in their final conclusions about extraordinary matters. As a result Zammit took time off from his law practice to research and write an online book titled, "A Lawyer Presents the Case for the Afterlife: Irrefutable Objective Evidence." In his book, Zammit shows proof of an afterlife from all angles skeptics typically criticize.

Victor Zammit, "A Lawyer Presents the Case for the Afterlife: Irrefutable Objective Evidence," www.victorzammit.com, 2000. Copyright © 2000 by Victor Zammit. Reproduced by permission.

There is undeniable scientific evidence to-day for the afterlife. I am an open-minded skeptic lawyer, a former practicing attorney-at-law formally qualified in a number of
university disciplines.

The argument that follows is not just an abstract, theoretical, academic legal argument. As an open-minded investigator, I set out to investigate the existing evidence for survival and with others to create conditions to test for
ourselves claims that communication with intelligences
from the afterlife is possible.

After many years of serious investigation I have come to
the irretrievable conclusion that there is a great body of evidence which taken as a whole absolutely and unqualifiedly
proves the case for the afterlife. I will not be arguing that the
objective evidence has just very high value. Nor am I suggesting that this evidence be accepted beyond reasonable
doubt. I am stating that the evidence *taken as a whole* con-
stitutes overwhelming and irrefutable proof for the existence of the afterlife. . . .

In absolute terms the evidence presented in this work will
convince the rational and intelligent open-minded skeptic
or the genuine searcher about the existence of the afterlife.

Scientific Observation of Mediums

Closed-minded skeptics have generally tried to down play
the achievements of mediums, suggesting that they are *all*
either outright frauds and cheats preying on the gullible or
mentally deluded.

While there are undoubtedly *some* who call themselves
'mediums' who have no talent and *some* who cheat and lie
for commercial purposes, there are also *some* genuine medi-

ums whose results have shocked the world with astonishingly accurate information obtained about the afterlife.

The general impression that materialist critics try to give the public is that *all* mediums work with vague suggestions, guesswork and astute observation of the client, or by 'mass hypnosis' of the audience.

However when one investigates the literature, using the same tests of credibility that historians use to ascertain whether certain events really happened, there is a staggering body of evidence which shows that there *have* been genuine mediums past and present who have amassed an amazing amount of objective evidence of survival of the individual personality.

A medium is a gifted person who communicates with beings from the afterlife. Mediumship covers many different types of psychic phenomena. The most common is 'mental mediumship' where the medium communicates through inner vision, clairaudience, automatic writing and automatic speech. Sometimes the medium goes totally into trance and another entity takes over the medium's body temporarily. There is also 'physical mediumship' which is characterized by rapping, levitation and movement of objects. Some rare physical mediums are able to produce 'direct voice' in which voices of departed loved ones speak to the audience without using the medium's vocal chords. Rarer still are 'materialization mediums' in whose presence objects and human and animal spirits actually appear.

John G. Fuller, a respected journalist who investigated the evidence on mediumship, points out the problem created by its sheer volume:

> On examination, it is so persuasive that it points to a rational conclusion that life is continuous, and that articulate communication is possible. One problem is that the evidence is piled so high that it is boring and tedious to go

through it. Like the study of mathematics and chemistry it requires painstaking labor to assess it (Fuller 1987: 67–68).

He points out that it took a committee of the Church of England two *years* to assess the great volume of the evidence on mediumship. The Committee was specially appointed in 1937 by Archbishop Lang and Archbishop Temple to investigate Spiritualism. Its investigations included sitting with some of the leading mediums in England. At the end of that time however seven of the ten members of the Committee—against enormous pressure—came to the conclusion that:

> the hypothesis that they (spirit communications) proceed in some cases from discarnate spirits is the true one (Psychic Press 1979).

This report was considered so dangerous by Church conservatives that it was stamped 'Private and Confidential' and locked away in Lambeth Palace for 40 years before it was leaked to the media in 1979.

Needle in the Haystack

It is extremely rare indeed to come across a very highly gifted psychic medium. George Meek, the American psychic researcher, spent 16 years traveling to different countries—from 1971 to 1987—trying to find the most gifted mediums in the world. In that time he found only six superb mediums, none of whom ever advertised their psychic abilities or charged money for their services (Meek 1987: 81–82).

We are told from the afterlife that the motives of a medium are very important to the maintenance and the quality of their mediumship—thus ego and desire to achieve status can actually lead to a reduction of the medium's powers and to the medium coming into contact with less developed spiritual beings.

When mediumship is used as a business there can be a

temptation to cheat or fake results when they don't come naturally and less developed spirits can be attracted. This means that while relatively lower intelligences can communicate through the medium, no great wisdom will be forthcoming. Materialism and spirituality are like oil and water—they don't mix.

In the West the great majority of truly gifted mediums have shunned publicity and have kept a deliberately low profile, taking little or no money and restricting their activities to small circles of trusted regular sitters. Recent history has taught genuine mediums to keep away from those calling themselves psychic researchers and to keep their work very private.

One medium who exemplified the ideal of mediumship as spiritual service was Chico Xavier of Brazil. Although poorly educated and almost blind he was the author of more than 126 spirit-dictated best selling books on a variety of highly specialized and technical subjects. However he renounced the wealth and influence which he was offered and dedicated his life and his mediumship to proving survival and to providing food, clothing and medical assistance for the poor. He was considered by many to be a radical Christian saint—a 'one man welfare system'—a man of 'almost pathological modesty and humility' (Playfair 1975: 27).

The literature of Spiritualism is full of self-published diaries and books attesting to wonderful events which have taken place and are continuing to take place through the work of such dedicated mediums. A recent book of this type is *Russel* (1994) in which the author Gwyne Byrne recounts how she and her husband Alf were reunited with their nine year old son who materialized through the mediumship of British Midlands medium Rita Goold on more than one hundred occasions. Gwyne has begun a society to comfort other parents whose children have 'died' called 'Russel's Pink Panther Society'. . . .

Many famous and hard-headed people have sat regularly with mediums for years and have published personal testimonies to what they have experienced first hand. One notable one was *Many Mansions*, first published in November 1943 by Air Chief Marshal Lord Dowding who led the British airforce in the Battle of Britain. Another was *Raymond*, written in 1916 by the leading British scientist of the day, Sir Oliver Lodge.

It was well known that Abraham Lincoln attended seances in the White House during the American Civil War and was lectured by a spirit being through an entranced medium on the necessity of freeing the slaves (Stemman 1975: 22–25). Queen Victoria, although nominally the head of the Church of England, for years communicated with her husband through John Brown, a trance medium, whom she had installed in her castle. She brought all her children up as spiritualists. Queen Elizabeth II often used the services of the medium Lillian Bailey to communicate with her late husband King George VI. Sir Winston Churchill was a close friend of the medium Bertha Harris during World War II. Bertha Harris had many Sunday evening visits to No 10 Downing Street during the war and predicted Pearl Harbor six months in advance of the attack (Meek 1973: 140). General Charles De Gaulle also consulted her regularly while he was in England during WWII after being introduced to her by Churchill (Meek 1973: 140).

And, according to Arthur Findlay, seances have been held in the Vatican. In *Looking Back* (1955) he recounts how in Rome in 1934 he addressed a large audience which included several high dignitaries of the Church. After the meeting he claims he was told by a cardinal that seances were held in the Vatican but that Pope Pius XI was a bad sitter and much better results were obtained when he was not present (Findlay 1955: 350).

A handful of mediums have co-operated with often hostile psychic researchers to demonstrate their gifts. Sometimes this has been at great personal cost since mediums are, by definition, people of highly developed sensitivity.

As was mentioned above, the Church of England conducted a two year study of mediumship in Britain in the 1930's. Its officials sat with some of the best mediums available and concluded that there was abundant evidence that good spirits could be contacted through mediumship and true guidance received.

Anyone wishing to disprove mediumship must deal with the evidence produced in this ten year study as well as the evidence produced by some of the world's best mediums referred to below.

A detailed investigation of the genuineness of mediumship was carried out by Professor Gary Schwartz and colleagues at the University of Arizona. Using well known mediums George Anderson and John Edward and lesser known mediums S. Northrop, L. Campbell and A. Gehman doing double blind studies, they found that the mediums were very accurate, to a degree far in excess of chance. The full first study was published in the *Journal of the Society of Psychical Research* in England in January, 2001. . . .

Answering the Closed-Minded Skeptics

In my dealings with people I have come across different groups—from those who readily accept the afterlife as a belief to others who are skeptics. I have had twenty-eight years experience dealing with non-believers. For nearly that long I was an open-minded skeptic myself.

An open-minded skeptic is someone who generally will not accept superstition or beliefs to explain physical or psychical phenomena. He or she will however accept scientifically and other objectively based results. . . . Many of the most famous psychic researchers began their investigations as open-minded skeptics.

I am on record for publicly articulating a skeptical view of life in the sense that I was not prepared to accept things I was told on 'faith'. I doubted, I questioned, I read, researched and I investigated.

I consider myself an *open-minded* skeptic—but not in the specific and the particular issue of the afterlife because I *thoroughly* investigated it.

Like many scientists, some of whom are regarded as 'giants' of science, who *bothered to systematically investigate* the afterlife, I too came to the irretrievable conclusion that we do survive physical death.

The evidence I was able to obtain myself for the existence of the afterlife is definitive, absolute, irrefutable and positively conclusive.

However, historically there are also what are known as closed-minded skeptics. The modern usage of the term 'closed-minded skeptic' in context of psychic phenomena, is someone who does not and will not accept the afterlife or the existence of psychic phenomena even if scientific proof is shown.

These people have already made up their minds about everything. And be they investigators or scholars, like the clergy in Galileo's time, they will refuse to consider even scientific information which contradicts their personal beliefs. They have extended the definition of 'skeptic' from 'one who doubts' to 'one who will never accept'.

The term 'closed-minded skeptic' as used in this book refers to this latter group.

Closed-minded skeptics who claimed they investigated psychic phenomena have mostly rejected the results of psychic experiments and observations, even when the results were objectively obtained. Their logic was that if the results proved positive, the experimenter must have been unqualified or in collusion with fraud because the afterlife and psychic phenomena do not exist and cannot exist. They took the role of prosecutor not investigator. Some of these unreasonably closed-minded skeptics have made most cowardly attacks on the lives and reputations of great men and women involved in psychic science and have been responsible for holding back knowledge of the afterlife for several decades. Many are still operating today, accepting large salaries and grants from the materialists to 'debunk' all things relating to the afterlife and psychic phenomena.

A classic comment which illustrates the inflexibility and the determination of the closed-minded skeptic to block any inconsistent new information was made at one of my meetings at the Humanists in Sydney, Australia. One hardcore, closed-minded skeptic burst out after I presented the objective evidence for the afterlife:

> I would not believe in the afterlife even if you could prove it to me, Victor!

Because of conscious and unconscious deletion, closed-minded skeptics only have some pieces of the jigsaw puzzle. They are NOT seeing the overall picture. Yet some of them have been rather vociferous about their unsubstantiable claim that the afterlife does not exist.

I concur with other empirical psychic researchers that even if the perfect demonstration of evidence for the existence of the afterlife—say, materialization of a loved one was witnessed by closed-minded skeptics, these skeptics would refuse to believe the evidence had anything to do with the afterlife.

Historically, *closed-minded* skeptics have opposed every invention and discovery and have made fools of themselves:

• Sir William Preece, former chief engineer of Britain's

Post Office, will be remembered for making one of the most 'idiotic' comments in history about Edison's inventions. Sir William stated that Edison's lamp (parallel circuit) was a *'completely idiotic idea'*!

• Professors, including Professor Henry Morton who knew Edison stated, immediately before Edison demonstrated the electric light globe: *'On behalf of science . . . Edison's experiments are a . . . fraud upon the public.'*

• The Scientific American, The New York Times, The New York Herald, the U.S. Army, academics—including Professor of Mathematics and Astronomy Simon Newcomb from Johns Hopkins University—and many other American scientists all heaped derision, ridicule and denigration onto the Wright brothers claiming that it was: *'scientifically impossible for machines to fly'*!

• One of the leading scientists from the French Academy of Sciences stated that hypnosis is a fraud and stated after seeing a hypnotized subject with a four inch needle in the top of his arm: *'This subject has been paid for not showing he's in pain.'*

• Another scientist from the French Academy of Sciences, after listening to a record made by Edison, stated: *'. . . clearly that is a case of ventriloquism'*!

• John Logie Baird, the inventor of television, was attacked by closed-minded skeptics who stated it was: *'absolute rubbish that television waves could produce a picture!'*. . .

What has to be remembered is that the belief of closed-minded skepticism is NOT scientific. Closed-minded skepticism does NOT have the substance of science to show that it is correct. On the contrary, closed-minded skepticism, like religion, as stated above, is a subjective belief and as a belief it is subject to fundamental error and to *complete invalidation*.

While there have been many eminent scientists who *after* investigating psychic phenomena did accept the existence for the afterlife, there has NEVER ever been any scientist in history—a physicist, biologist, geologist, astronomer or anybody else—who could prove that the afterlife does *not* exist and there will never be.

The rational and informed searcher will reject the world conspiracy theory—that all those highly accredited scientists in different countries who have worked to show that the afterlife exists got together over the last one hundred years or so to fool the rest of the world.

The afterlife is inevitable and the consequences of it are enormous.

Rebutting the Skeptics on EVP and ITC

What do the hardcore skeptics say about electronic voice phenomena?

Of the objections raised by the skeptics I quote a leading representative of the hardcore skeptics, an Assistant Professor of Psychology at Pace University in the United States, Professor Hines. In his book called *Pseudoscience And The Paranormal—a Critical Examination of the Evidence* (1987) we are told the following on page 76. Remember, this hardcore skeptic explicitly claims that his work is supposed to be a *'critical examination of the evidence'.*

> . . . if one takes a tape recorder out to a graveyard one can record the voices of the dead. How? Put the machine in the 'record' mode with a blank tape and turn the volume all the way up. Then, when you play the tape back, if you listen carefully, you'll hear the voices of the dead. They're not very clear, to be sure, but if you listen long and carefully, you can begin to make them out . . . the tape recording . . . is picking up stray sounds from the environment and especially, the sound of the breeze or wind passing over the microphone . . .

> If one expects to hear voices, constructive perception will produce voices . . . the Indians used to believe that the dead spoke as the wind swirled through the trees. The tape recorder has simply brought this illusion into a technological age (Hines 1987: 76).

Now here was the opportunity for this assistant professor to identify the classic research done by some of the world's top scholars and others and to issue a credible scholarly rebuttal of the research on a scientific basis. He *was* expected to scientifically scrutinize the research of Dr Raudive in Germany, Friedrich Jurgenson in Sweden, Peter Bander in England, Marcello Bacci in Grosseto, Italy, Professor Walter & others such as George Meek in the United States, to name just a few.

The scientists and other reputable researchers mentioned do not go to 'the graveyard'. They usually work in carefully controlled conditions in laboratories with other observers who include amongst them some skeptics, atheists, journalists, clergymen, psychics. Sometimes they work in professional recording studios as with Dr Peter Bander's sessions.

The voices are clearly not auditory hallucinations—they have been heard by rooms full of people and by millions of people across Europe at the same time. Thousands of voices have been identified, recorded and corroborated by independent witnesses. Much of the subject matter has been checked and found to be factual. Electronic voice-pattern analysis has matched the voices to those of the person while alive.

Why did this Assistant Professor not deal with any of the evidence, starting with say, the contents of Dr Raudive's international book *Breakthrough*? Technically, when evidence for the afterlife is presented by the assertor, the onus shifts onto the other party not accepting the evidence to argue on what technical basis the evidence is not accepted.

This Assistant Professor should have examined some of the best 'spirit voices' of the 72,000 voices taped by Dr Raudive such as the voice of Raudive's own secretary Margarete Petrautski who called out Raudive's wife's name 'Zenta' and identified herself as 'Margarete'. She then went on to say: 'Imagine, I really exist!'—English translation from German,

'Bedenke ich bin' (Bander 1973: 25).

Assistant Professor Hines should explain:

- why the apparent voices were not really voices,
- if it is admitted that they were voices, why they were not those of the dead.

He should have taken a sample of this Margarete Petrautski's voice and compared it with the tape recording of her voice before her death as the researchers did. Highly sophisticated voice machines exist to-day which can accurately and scientifically measure all voice variables, eg, pace, rhythm, accents, origin, etc. The Margarete Petrautski tapes are excellent subjects for scientific scrutiny because of the exceptionally good quality recordings of her voice. Yet this Assistant Professor chose to ignore scientific method and fall back on his closed-minded entrenched skepticism.

If the Assistant Professor endeavored to adhere to scientific method and showed in some way that he could be technically correct, or that the evidence presented should not be accepted, identifying the project as subjective, one would perhaps discuss the project with him and explore the voices to ascertain where the voices could be coming from.

But he didn't. Assistant Professor Hines chose **not** to identify the classical scientific work done and being done on the EVP on a global scale because he knows this scientific work is substantive and cannot be rebutted. He resorted to technical cheating because he knows that Electronic Voice Phenomena is powerful in objectively proving the existence of the afterlife.

To push this argument further, instead of launching a scientific investigation to rebut the Voice Phenomena, this Assistant Professor has fraudulently made something up, deliberately indulged in willful lies to try to fool the reader by deceitfully concocting false information to make it compatible with his own skeptical non-scientific partiality.

Whilst to some people the blatant omission may seem quite odd, to others the total omission of the closed-minded skeptics to include any criticism of the Electronic Voice Phenomena in their books is not a surprise at all.

As we have already seen, those researchers in the Electronic Voice Phenomena who used scientific method to present the evidence for the afterlife have successfully made their case.

In scientific method, as in formal logic, if anyone does not formally rebut the evidence produced, then the scientific evidence stands as absolutely valid until it is rebutted—if ever it can be rebutted. That is a fundamental scientific premise.

My experience with closed-minded skeptics however is that some will never listen to reason. Some will refuse to add the 7 + 5 and therefore will not even endeavor to discuss the result 12. Further I state that it is a waste of time and energy discussing anything with the closed-minded skeptics—they do not appear to have the capacity to be impartial or to rebut the evidence or to substantiate their claims in any way whatsoever.

And whilst Electronic Voice Phenomena and Instrumental Transcommunication have not yet been perfected, it does not mean that the scientific evidence collected thus far from the EVP and ITC does not exist!

For the agnostic or the skeptic or the non-believer, the voices captured on tape recorders making sharp responses to specific questions are in absolute and unequivocal terms the voices of people who have 'died' and moved on to the next world.

Unequivocally, communicating with intelligences from the afterlife is indeed the greatest discovery ever made. The consequences of the information being transmitted are enormous!

Scientific Experiments Prove Life After Death Communications

Gary E. Schwartz, Linda Russek, Lonnie Nelson, and Christopher Barensten

Psychic mediums have been claiming to speak to the dead since 1834 when the Fox sisters claimed to communicate with the dead through rapping on walls. The means of communicating with the dead have become more sophisticated, however until recently there was not a sophisticated method of testing the claims scientifically. Gary E. Schwartz was the first to test a psychic medium's validity through scientific methods.

Dr. Schwartz was initially contacted by HBO to conduct such a study to be used for an after-death communications documentary. With proper funding, Schwartz and his colleagues were able to conduct a scientific study in a controlled laboratory.

Gary E. Schwartz, Linda Russek, Lonnie Nelson, and Christopher Barensten, "Accuracy and Replicability of Anomalous After-Death Communication Across Highly Skilled Mediums," *Journal of the Society for Psychical Research*, 2001. Copyright © 2001 by Gary E. Schwartz. Reproduced by permission.

Dr. Schwartz and his colleagues were convinced after the scientific study that psychic mediums were communicating with the dead. He published his findings in a book titled: *The Afterlife Experiments*. The following is a summary of his findings.

Empirical research on mediumship has been limited by a number of factors:

(1) availability of experienced mediums willing to collaborate in research

(2) availability of subjects (sitters) willing to engage in careful scoring of transcripts, and funding to investigate these questions.

The research reported here became possible through unique circumstances. A major US television network decided to produce a documentary on after-death communication (ADC) and the plausibility of survival of consciousness after physical death. When the producer/director (Lisa Jackson) approached Gary Schwartz and his wife, Linda Russek, about possibly participating in the documentary, it was proposed that if they were seriously interested in the science of mediumship, they should fund a first-ever laboratory experiment with well known mediums to examine possible inter-medium replicability of information obtained during readings under controlled circumstances. Moreover, thanks to the interest and cooperation of the mediums whose data are reported here, it was possible to record 19 channels of EEG and ECGs from each of them as well as from one of the sitters.

The data were collected in the Human Energy Systems Laboratory at the University of Arizona in Tucson. Preliminary analyses were reported at the June 1999 meeting of the

Society for Scientific Exploration and were shown in the HBO special "Life Afterlife" which was broadcast in October 1999. Subsequent detailed scoring and analyses are reported here.

A replication and extension experiment was conducted. Four of the five original mediums were able to coordinate their schedules to participate in the research. Unique circumstances occurred again. The husband of the sitter featured in the HBO documentary died a few days before the replication and extension experiment was to be conducted. The design of the second experiment made it possible to collect data in such a way that the mediums would not be able to identify the sitters. The sitter agreed to be "re-read" to see if information could be replicated and extended to include the death of her husband. Hence, replicability of information was addressed not only across five mediums (Experiment I, the HBO experiment), but over time as well for two of the mediums (Experiment II, the Miraval experiment). The replication and extension experiment was made possible by support from Canyon Ranch Resort, the Miraval Resort, the Susy Smith Project from the University of Arizona, and the Family Love and Health Foundation. The data were collected at Miraval in Tucson. . . .

The HBO Experiment

Purpose

The primary purpose of the HBO Experiment was to determine whether mediums could independently obtain accurate and replicable information from a sitter under controlled naturalistic conditions. . . .

The secondary purpose was exploratory. The purpose was to examine possible ECG/ECG and ECG/EEG synchrony between mediums and a sitter during baseline and reading periods. We hypothesized that if mediums were engaged in either psychological (focused attention) and/or parapsychological reading (telepathy) of the sitter (i.e. the physically living), increased evidence of ECG/ECG and ECG/EEG medium-sitter synchrony might be observed during the readings compared to resting baselines (Russek and Schwartz, 1994; Song, Schwartz, and Russek, 1998). However, if the mediums were focusing their attention away from the sitter (e.g. attending to communication from the departed), decreased ECG/ECG and/or ECG/EEG medium-sitter synchrony might be observed during the readings compared to resting baselines. . . .

Mediums

Four internationally known mediums agreed to come to Tucson to collaborate in the research: listed alphabetically, George Anderson, John Edward, Anne Gehman, and Suzane Northrop. The fifth, Laurie Campbell, had previously participated in mediumship research conducted in our laboratory (Schwartz et al, 1999; Schwartz and Russek, 1999).

The mediums were fully informed that the Human Energy Systems Laboratory was collaborating with HBO, that the research would be professionally filmed and aired internationally, that the research required they be blind to the identity of the sitters selected for the research, and that the research required the highest integrity of all involved—the laboratory, HBO, the mediums, and the sitters.

Sitters

Each of the five mediums had an experimental session with one sitter, a 46 year old woman who lives north of Tucson. She was selected because she had experienced the death of at least six loved ones in the past ten years. The sitter was recruited by HBO. The sitter was recommended to HBO by an ADC researcher who knew of her case. HBO informed the sitter that it was essential that her identity be kept secret from the mediums until after the experiment was completed. Moreover, she was told that her identity would be kept secret from the researchers until the day before the experiment was to be conducted.

A second woman personally known by G.E.R.S. and L.G.S.R. (a 54 year old woman who lives in Tucson who had also experienced the death of at least six loved ones in the past ten years) was invited to serve as the second sitter. The identity of this sitter was kept secret from HBO as well as the mediums. Time permitted collecting experimental sessions with the second sitter and two of the mediums.

Both sitters signed statements indicating that they had no verbal or written contact with any of the five mediums prior to the experiment.

Information about the sitters were kept secret from the mediums. They only knew that each of the sitters had experienced the loss of multiple loved ones in a ten year period.

Measures

Pretest information was obtained about each of the six deceased individuals that each sitter predicted might be received by one or more of the mediums (Appendix B).

During the experimental readings, the sitters took notes. Immediately after each reading, they completed numeric ratings from -1 to +5 (Appendix C).

Each of the five mediums and one of the sitters were fitted with an electrode cap containing 19 EEG electrodes and a ground. Linked ear electrodes were attached as well as ECG recorded arm to arm. The electrodes were attached by Lonnie Nelson and Mercy Fernandez, Ph.D. using standard electrode paste and impedance reducing procedures; all electrode resistances were less than 5 K ohms.

The EEG and ECG signals were recorded on two Lexicor Neurosearch 24 systems and processed by PCs, one system for the medium and a second system for the sitter. The signals were sampled at 256 Hz. The ECG signals from the mediums and the sitter were recorded in both systems. Using specially designed software, it was possible to examine ECG-triggered signal-averaging within the mediums and sitter (intrapersonal ECG/EEG interactions) and between the mediums and sitter (interpersonal ECG/ECG and ECG/EEG interactions) (Russek and Schwartz, 1994; Song, Schwartz, and Russek, 1998).

A few months after the data were collected, each of the sitters was invited back individually to the laboratory to carefully score transcripts of each of the mediums obtained from the video recordings. Every possible item uttered by each of the mediums was placed in one of six categories (name, initial, historical fact, personal description, temperament, and "opinion") and rated by the sitter using a numeric scale (-3 definitely an error, -2 probably an error, -1 possibly an error, 0 maybe an error or maybe correct, +1 possibly correct, +2 probably correct, +3 definitely correct).

The sitters were required to explain and justify each accuracy rating that they made for the items. Justification of accuracy ratings, particularly +3's, could be as simple as "my deceased son's name was Michael" (name category) to as complex as "my grandmother did have false teeth, and she did take them in and out in public, which greatly embarrassed my mother" (historical fact category).

The sitters were also required to indicate whether the information could be independently verified by another living family member or friend (only the "opinion" category contained items that could not be independently verified).

Each item was read out loud by G.E.R.S.; the ratings were recorded in Excel files by C.B. The experimenters repeatedly emphasized the research requirement of rating accuracy and possible verification (given the specific nature of the content, none was performed).

Note that ratings of accuracy do not discriminate between differences in degree of specificity. For example, accurate information such as "M" (initial), "Michael" (name), "committed suicide" (historical fact), "thin" (personal description), "playful sense of humor" (temperament), and "does not blame you for his decision to kill himself" (opinion) differ in their degree of specificity, but they were all correct and received accuracy ratings of +3 by a sitter.

Procedure

Seven data collection sessions (five for sitter one and two for sitter two) were collected in the energy cardiology laboratory of the Human Energy Systems Laboratory in the course of a single day. The data were collected in February, 1999. Each session took approximately one hour (including lead connecting and disconnecting, file naming on the computers, baselines, and readings). The room was arranged to accommodate the experimental design as well as the needs for filming. The two EEG/ECG systems were placed furthest from the door (run by G.E.R.S.). The sitter sat in a comfortable chair adjacent to the recording equipment, in view of G.E.R.S. and two video cameras run by the HBO filming team. Each medium entered the room, one per session, and sat down in a comfortable chair which was separated from the sitter's chair by a large floor standing cloth covered screen. The screen was approximately 6 feet high by 4 feet wide. Though the medium was never visible to the sitter during the reading, and vice versa, the medium was visible to both video cameras, as was the sitter.

Each medium was run individually, the order of their participation selected by agreement from all five mediums. The mediums waited their turn in the courtyard behind the laboratory and were closely and continuously monitored throughout the day by one of the senior investigators plus a research assistant to insure that no communication about the sessions occurred during the day of data collection. As mentioned previously, the mediums understood that integrity was absolutely essential in this research, and that fraud would not be tolerated during the experiment.

When each medium entered the room, their ECG and EEG leads were connected to the Lexicor. A two minute eyes closed resting baseline was obtained for both the medium and the sitter. Following the resting baseline, each medium briefly explained to the sitter how she or he conducted a reading. Then the medium was allowed to conduct the reading in her or his own way, with the restriction that they could ask only yes or no questions. The mediums varied in the number of questions they asked. The actual reading lasted for approximately 15 to 20 minutes.

After the reading was completed, the medium left the experimental room and returned to the courtyard. The experimenter reminded each medium not to discuss the reading(s) until the experiment was completed, and that they would be continuously monitored by two experimenters. The sitters then made their immediate ratings as follows:

Results

Sitter 1 (5 Readings): Immediate Ratings

The immediate ratings, though important, are not primary, and therefore are noted only briefly here. The major findings are the detailed scoring results reported in the next section.

The number of departed persons identified by the sitter (based upon her original list of 6) for each of the five mediums were 5, 4, 3, 3, and 4 respectively; the resemblance ratings ranged from 4 to 5+ (verifiable names, dates, causes of death, personal characteristics, etc.). The average percent identification was 63%.

Interestingly, according to the sitter, each of the five mediums independently communicated specific information from 2 of the 6 departed individuals on her original list (the sitter's mother and son). Hence, one third of the anticipated departed persons were independently replicated 100% across all five mediums.

In addition, anomalous information from 9 other departed individuals (not on the original list of 6) was also documented. The numbers of additional departed persons identified by the sitter from her readings with each of the five mediums were 5, 6, 1, 5, 4; the resemblance ratings ranged from 4 to 5.

According to the sitter, specific information identifying two of these individuals (the sitter's grandfather, and a dog beloved by her deceased son) were independently communicated by four of the five mediums. Hence, two of the unexpected departed individuals were replicated 80% across the mediums.

In light of these initial summary observations, careful item by item ratings of the transcripts were conducted.

Sitter 1 (5 Ratings): Item by Item Yes/No Answers

Figure 1 displays the total number of items per reading,

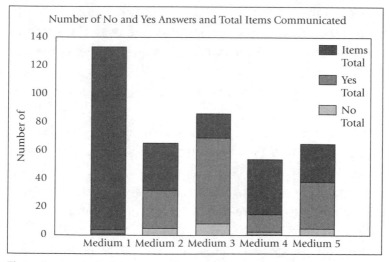

Figure 1

the number of questions asked that received a yes answer, and the number of questions asked that received a no answer.

Figure 2 displays the percentage of questions asked to the total number of items generated.

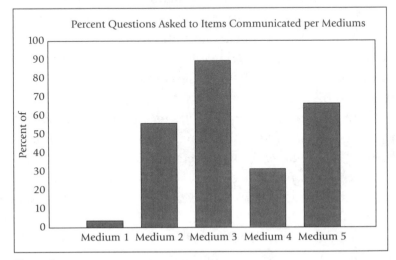

Figure 2

It can be seen that the mediums varied in the number of total items they obtained and the number of questions they asked. Medium 1, in particular, generated over 130 specific pieces of information yet asked only 5 questions, 4 of which (80%) were answered yes.

Figure 3 displays the percentage of yes answers obtained per medium.

The five mediums ranged in percent yes answers, the average accuracy was 85%. Medium 1, who obtained the lowest score (80%), only asked a total of five questions. Hence, it is impossible to claim that medium 1's percent accuracy ratings (see below) were due to "cold reading" and "fishing for information."

However, the question arose, did the other mediums obtain their high accuracy scores because they asked more

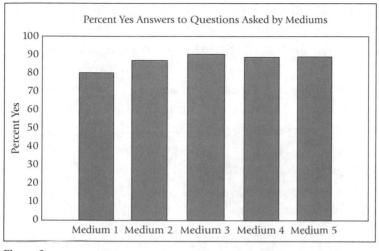

Figure 3

questions. To address this question, the data were analyzed just for the first five questions asked. The results are displayed in Figure 4.

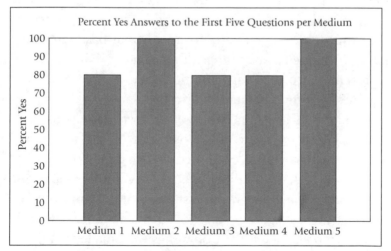

Figure 4

It can be seen that accuracy ranged from 80% to 100%, the average was 88%. A chi square comparing the number of yes versus no answers for the first five questions, compared with a simple, binary (yes/no) estimate of chance (50%) was p<.006. It is unclear whether the use of a simple binary 50% estimate over or under estimates chance in this experiment. A careful analysis of the content suggests that the 50% figure may be an over estimation. The first thirteen questions of medium 3 are presented verbatim in the general discussion to illustrate the nature of the content of the yes/no questions and their degree of specificity and precision.

The data suggest that according to the sitter's ratings, the mediums were receiving accurate information.

Comparison to Base Rate Guessing—The Numeric Accuracy Ratings

The question arises, can intelligent and motivated persons guess this kind of information by chance alone? Some items were yes/no (e.g. is your son alive or dead?), other items were less susceptible to probability estimation (e.g. does your son's first name begin with the letter ____?). Since it was impossible to estimate ahead of time base rates per item, we selected a large range of representative items, both correct and incorrect, and obtained control subject's guessing rates for sitter 1's data empirically.

A questionnaire containing 70 representative items was created, based on the content provided by the mediums. Some items were yes/no, others required that subjects provide content answers. It was administrated to a control group of 68 male and female undergraduate students at the University of Arizona (average age 21 years, 70% female). Since it would have been preferable if control ratings were made by a large group of middle aged female subjects who were matched to the demographics of the sitters, the control findings reported here should be viewed with some caution.

The control subjects were challenged to try and guess as

well as the mediums did. As an incentive, they were told that after they completed the questionnaires, they would be told what the actual answers were, and then they would be able to watch the HBO documentary.

The data are displayed in Figure 5.

Their average accuracy for the 70 items was 36%, ranging from 20% to 54%. The mediums average accuracy score (+3 ratings out of the total number of items receiving a rating per medium) was 83%, ranging from 77% to 93%. Especially significant is that Medium 1, who asked only 5 questions, received 83% ratings of +3 out of Medium 1's total of 130 items. A test comparing the performance of the mediums versus the control group was p less than one in ten million. . . .

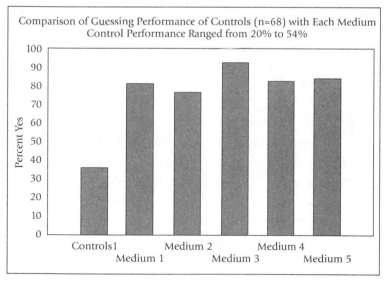

Figure 5

Conclusion

It appears that highly skilled mediums, in laboratory controlled yet supportive conditions, can receive specific categories of information that can be rated accurately by trained research sitters. One sitter had independent readings with five mediums. She also had her ECG and EEG recorded. The other sitter had separate readings with two of the five mediums. The average percent accuracy was 83% for the first sitter and 77% for the second sitter. Each of the mediums performed well above guessing rates. Control subjects who attempted to guess the information averaged 36% accuracy for all categories of information combined. The p value was less than one in ten million.

The percent guessing accuracy of the control subjects may be somewhat lower than the actual guessing accuracy because (1) the control subjects were substantially younger than the sitters (older subjects might have more extended information to guess from) and (2) they did not have the benefit of hearing the answers to the yes/no questions like the mediums did. On the other hand, the control subjects were shown a picture of the woman (the mediums did not see the sitters until after all the data were collected). Given the clearly specific nature of the representative items, it seems improbable that a second group of control subjects who were matched for age, sex, and demographics, even given yes/no feedback per answer, would score as high as the mediums did in this experiment by guessing per se. . . .

The preliminary ECG and EEG findings are intriguing and worth exploring in future research. No evidence was found for mediums registering the sitter's ECG in their EEG's. Moreover, when the readings began, the degree of heart to heart synchrony between the medium and sitter changed—the medium's heart tended to beat when the sitter's heart was not beating. The combination of the ECG and EEG findings are not consistent with the telepathy hypothesis that the mediums were registering the energy or memories of the sitter. The pattern of findings are consistent with the hypothesis that these mediums may be disconnecting biophysically from the sitter as they attempt to receive anomalous communication, purportedly from departed individuals. Qualitative data presented in the general discussion also suggests that telepathy with the sitter does not satisfactorily account for all the findings.

The purpose of including the preliminary EKG/EEG data in this report is to illustrate the potential of using such techniques in future research to address possible biophysical mechanisms of anomalous information retrieval. Future research will require the use of appropriate control conditions comparing, for example, non-mediumistic versus mediumistic communication periods, to draw definitive conclusions about the meaning of the cardiac findings observed in Experiment I. . . .

The Miraval Experiment

Purpose

The Miraval Experiment was designed to attempt to replicate and extend the HBO Experiment. The primary purpose was (1) to use a new group of sitters from various parts of the country who varied in age, sex, history of number of personal losses, belief in the plausibility of after-death communication, and depth of love for the departed, and (2) to add a new control condition that did not allow any verbal communication between the medium and the sitter.

Mediums

Four of the original five mediums were able to come to Tucson to collaborate in the research: listed alphabetically, Laurie Campbell, John Edward, Anne Gehman, and Suzane Northrop.

The Sitter

This report presents the findings from sitter one, whose husband died in a car crash a few days before the Miraval Experiment was to be conducted in June, 1999. She called

L.G.S.R. to share her loss. L.G.S.R. suggested that she might consider being a sitter in the upcoming Miraval Experiment, since Part I occurred in complete silence, and the sitters could not be seen by the mediums. This remarkable coincidence led to the replication data reported here. The sitter affirmed that she had no verbal or written contact with any of the mediums about the death of her husband and her subsequent participation in the Miraval Experiment.

Procedure

The four mediums were housed at Canyon Ranch which is located more than ten miles from Miraval. The sitter was housed in a separate hotel. Testing was conducted over two days. The four mediums were taken to four separate rooms, each room was separated by at least four other rooms. There were four experimenters. The sitters were sequestered in a separate room, many rooms away from where the mediums were being tested. The mediums sat in a comfortable chair, facing a video camera and backup audio tape recorder, with their backs to the door. A given experimenter would enter the room, make sure that the medium was seated with her or his back to the door and facing the video recorder. The tape recorders would then be started. Next, the sitter was brought into the room and seated approximately six feet behind the medium.

For the first ten minutes, the mediums were instructed to receive whatever information they could about the deceased and share this information out loud. They were not allowed to ask any questions of the sitters. The sitters were instructed to remain silent. After this Part I silent period, the mediums were allowed to ask yes/no questions, replicating the procedure used in Experiment I.

The sitter reported here was brought in to participate at the end of the two days; time permitted that she could be read by mediums 1 and 2 from the HBO Experiment who also participated in the Miraval Experiment. Gary Schwartz was the experimenter. The sessions were taped, and the verbal information transcribed.

Results

The content of these two readings was dramatic. Information about the deceased son and dog were again replicated by both mediums. However, both mediums also received information about the recently deceased husband. Medium 2 reported being confused, saying "I keep hearing Michael times two, Michael times two." The father's name was Michael, the son's name was Michael, Jr.

A few months after these two sessions, after the transcripts had been prepared, the sitter returned to the laboratory for a detailed scoring session. The five hour scoring session was recorded on video tape. G.E.R.S. again read the items out loud, and C.B. recorded the answers in an Excel file. The rating procedure was identical to Experiment 1, using numbers from -3 to +3.

Figure 6 displays the summary findings.

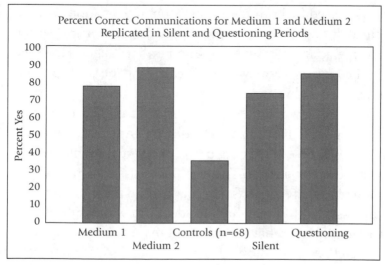

Figure 6

The two left bars display the percent +3 accuracy ratings for medium1 and medium 2, combining the data for the silent (Part I) and questioning (Part II) periods. It can be seen that the average accuracy for the two mediums was 82%. Medium 1 generated a total of 127 items, medium 2 a total of 94 items.

The two right bars display the percent + accuracy ratings for the silent and questioning periods, combining the data for mediums 1 and 2. The average accuracy for the silent periods was 77% and for the questioning period, 85%. The total number of items received during the silent period was 64, the total during the questioning period was 157. The difference between the silent and questioning periods in percent accuracy was not statistically significant. The control subject's percent accuracy ratings from Experiment I are included in the center for comparison. . . .

Discussion

The accuracy of mediums 1 and 2 was replicated, including during a ten minute silent period when no questioning was allowed. New information about the deceased husband was received by both mediums. More information was obtained during the questioning period than the silent period, and the accuracy ratings were somewhat higher. However, detailed information was obtained during the silent periods when no "cold reading" was possible. . . .

Interestingly and surprisingly, neither medium reported guessing who the sitter was during or immediately following the yes/no questioning period. The experimenter would not allow the mediums to see the sitter until he pressed them repeatedly to guess who was behind them. Both mediums insisted that they had no idea who was behind them. They both stated that they conduct many readings per week in their busy professional lives and that it is difficult to keep specific readings straight in their minds, especially after many months. Both expressed profound shock when they were allowed to see the sitter and recognized her from the HBO Experiment. It should be recalled that the mediums had not been told what had happened to this sitter by Russek or Schwartz, and that they had not been told that they would be "re-reading" her in the replication and extension experiment. Their sadness visibly increased when they realized that it was her husband, Michael senior, who had recently died.

An anonymous reviewer suggested the interesting possibility that the mediums might have recognized the sitter's odor unconsciously which triggered memories of their prior readings. This suggestion is creative but does not explain all of the data. For example, in the HBO Experiment, medium 1 reported seeing a little brown dog. In The Miraval Experiment, medium 1 reported seeing a spotted beagle. After the session, the sitter explained that the mother of the brown dog experienced by four of the mediums in the HBO Experiment was indeed a spotted beagle. At the rating session a few months later, the sitter brought photos of both the spotted beagle (the mother) and the little brown dog (her offspring).

General Discussion—Quantitative Findings

These two experiments provide quantitative data that are consistent with the hypothesis that some form of anomalous information retrieval was occurring in these skilled mediums. Traditional hypotheses of fraud, subtle cueing, and statistical coincidence, are improbable explanations of the total set of observations reported here. Adopting William James's metaphor, the particular mediums participating in this research may be examples of five "white crows" of anomalous information retrieval.

The experimenters have not ruled out definitively that

HBO, with or without the cooperation of sitter 1, engaged in deception in Experiment I. Private detectives were not employed to attempt to independently verify confidentiality. However, it seems highly improbable that Lisa Jackson, an Emmy Award winning Producer who works for a multiple Emmy Award winning production company, would risk her professional and personal reputation, as well as the reputation of her production company, to engage in fraud at the University of Arizona. Moreover, the experimenters had independently selected a second sitter whose identity was kept secret from HBO as well as from the mediums. Lisa Jackson and her team was well aware of the consequences of risking their integrity as well as the integrity of the laboratory. The experimenters were sensitive to the unique nature of this research and the need to eliminate, as best as possible, the occurrence of deception in the experiments. This included having the mediums watched at all times by two experimenters in the HBO Experiment to insure that the mediums were reminded of the absolute requirement for integrity.

The present findings do not speak directly to the mechanism(s) of anomalous information retrieval observed. However, the apparent desynchrony of the medium's ECG's with the sitter's ECG during the reading periods compared to the baseline periods is inconsistent with a "telepathy with the sitter" interpretation of the findings. If telepathy with the sitter was involved, increased medium-sitter ECG/ECG synchrony might have been observed. Interpersonal medium-sitter ECG/ECG and ECG/EEG measurements may be useful in future research on possible mechanisms of mediumship phenomena (Russek and Schwartz, 1994).

References

Braude, S. E. (1992). Survival or super-psi? Journal of Scientific Exploration. 6,2: 127–144.

Cook, E.W., Greyson, B., & Stevenson, I. (1998). Do any near-death experiences provide evidence for the survival of human personality after death? Relevant features and illustrative case reports. Journal of Scientific Exploration. 12,3: 3737–406.

Russek, L.G. and Schwartz, G.E. (1994). Interpersonal Heart-Brain Registration and the Perception of Parental Love: A 42 Year Follow-up of the Harvard Mastery of Stress Study. Subtle Energies. 5,3: 195–208.

Schwartz, G.E.R. and Russek, L.G.S. (1999). The Living Energy Universe: A Fundamental Discovery that Transforms Science and Medicine. Charlottesville, VA: Hampton Roads Publishing.

Schwartz, G.E.R., Russek, L.G.S., et al. (1999). Potential Medium to Departed to Medium Communication of Pictorial Information: Exploratory Evidence Consistent with Psi and Survival of Consciousness. The Noetics Journal, in press.

Song, L.Z.Y.X., Schwartz, G.E.R., and Russek L.G.R. (1998). Heart-focused attention and heart-brain synchronization: Energetic and physiological mechanisms. Alternative Therapies in Health and Medicine. 4,5: 44–63.

Instructions for "Sitters":

After each "sitting" with each medium, rate the medium on how accurate he or she was in receiving information from each of your deceased friends or relatives. Use the following numbers to rate your overall impression per deceased friend or relative:

-1 Mistaken identity
1 No mention
2 Slight resemblance
3 Moderate resemblance
4 Strong resemblance
5 Very strong resemblance
6 Definite communication
Deceased
Person
Medium 1 Medium 2 Medium 3 Medium 4 Medium 5
(fill in names)

Past-Life Hypnotic Regression Proves Life After Death

Michael Newton

Hypnosis has been around throughout the ages. It has been described on stone walls in ancient Egypt. Ancient fathers of Chinese medicine wrote about hypnotic techniques. There are also biblical references to hypnosis in the Old and New Testaments.

Today hypnosis is still used, primarily by psychologists to help people recall traumatic events buried in the unconscious or to aid people in stopping negative behaviors, such as smoking or overeating. Another lesser-known use of hypnosis is to take a subject back in time, back to a previous life. This technique, known as past-life regression, is practiced by some psychologists to help patients understand who they are today by understanding who they were in another life.

If people are able to experience a previous life, it would prove life after death. Michael Newton holds a Ph.D. in counseling psychology and is a master hypnotherapist. According to Newton, his experiences with many patients have enabled him to uncover the secrets of life after death. In the following article, Newton explains the process a soul takes after the death of the physical body. He also explains why he believes in life after death.

At the moment of death, our soul rises out of its host body. If the soul is older and has experience from many former lives, it knows immediately it has been set free and is going home. These advanced souls need no one to greet them. However, most souls I work with are met by guides just outside Earth's astral plane. A young soul, or a child who has died, may be a little disoriented until someone comes closer to ground level for them. There are souls who choose to remain at the scene of their death for a while. Most wish to leave at once. Time has no meaning in the spirit world. Discarnates who choose to comfort someone who is grieving, or have other reasons to stay near the place of their death for a while, experience no sense of time loss. This becomes *now* time for the soul as opposed to linear time.

As they move further away from Earth, souls experience an increasingly brilliant light around them. Some will briefly see a grayish darkness and will sense passing through a tunnel or portal. The differences between these two phenomena depends upon the exit speed of the soul, which in turn relates to their experience. The pulling sensation from our guides may be gentle or forceful depending upon the soul's maturity and capacity for rapid change. In the early stages of their exit all souls encounter a "wispy cloudiness" around them that soon becomes clear, enabling them to look off into a vast distance. This is the moment when the average soul sees a ghostly form of energy coming toward them. This figure may be a loving soulmate or two, but more often than not it is our guide. In circumstances where we are met by a spouse or friend who has passed on before us, our guide is also close by so they can take over the transition process. In all my years of research, I have never had a single subject who was met by a major religious figure such as Jesus or Buddha. Still, the loving essence of the great teachers from Earth is within the personal guides who are assigned to us.

A Soul's Makeup

By the time souls become reoriented again to the place they call home, their earthliness has changed. They are no longer quite human in the way we think of a human being with a particular emotional, temperamental and physical makeup. For instance, they don't grieve about their recent physical death in the way their loved ones will. It is our souls that make us human on Earth, but without our bodies we are no longer *Homo sapiens*. The soul has such majesty that it is beyond description. I tend to think of souls as intelligent light forms of energy. Right after death, souls suddenly feel different because they are no longer encumbered by a temporary host body with a brain and central nervous system. Some take longer to adjust than others.

The energy of the soul is able to divide into identical parts, similar to a hologram. It may live parallel lives in other bodies although this is much less common than we read about. However, because of the dual capability of all souls, part of our light energy always remains behind in the spirit world. Thus, it is possible to see your mother upon returning from a life even though she may have died thirty Earth years before and reincarnated again.

Orientation periods with our guides, which take place before joining our cluster group, vary between souls and between different lives for the same soul. This is a quiet time for counseling, with the opportunity to vent any frustrations we have about the life just ended. Orientation is intended to be an initial debriefing session with gentle probing by perceptive, caring teacher-guides.

The meeting may be long or short depending upon the circumstances of what we did or did not accomplish with regard to our life contract. Special karmic issues are also reviewed, although, they will be discussed later in minute detail within our soul cluster group. The returning energy of some souls will not be sent back into their soul group right away. These are the souls who were contaminated by their physical bodies and became involved with evil acts. There is a difference between wrongdoing with no premeditated desire to hurt someone and intentional evil. The degrees of harm to others from mischief to malevolence are carefully evaluated.

Evil and Worn-Out Spirits

Those souls who have been associated with evil are taken to special centers which some clients call "intensive care units." Here, I am told, their energy is remodeled to make it whole again. Depending upon the nature of their transgressions, these souls could be rather quickly returned to Earth. They might well choose to serve as the victims of other's evil acts in the next life. Still, if their actions were prolonged and especially cruel over a number of lives, this would denote a pattern of wrongful behavior. Such souls could spend a long while in a solitary spiritual existence, possibly over a thousand Earth years. A guiding principle in the spirit world is that wrongdoing, intentional or unintentional, on the part of all souls will need to be redressed in some form in a future life. This is not considered punishment or even penance as much as an opportunity for karmic growth.

There is no hell for souls, except perhaps on Earth.

Some lives are so difficult that the soul arrives home very tired. Despite the energy rejuvenation process initiated by our guides who combine their energy with ours at the gateway, we may still have a depleted energy flow. In these cases, more rest and solitude may be called for rather than celebrations. Indeed, many souls who desire rest receive it before reunification with their groups. Our soul groups may be boisterous or subdued, but they are respectful of what we have gone through during an incarnation. All groups welcome back their friends in their own way with deep love and camaraderie.

The Reunion with Soulmates

Homecoming is a joyous interlude, especially following a physical life where there might not have been much karmic contact with our intimate soulmates. Most of my subjects tell me they are welcomed back with hugs, laughter and much humor, which I find to be a hallmark of life in the spirit world. The really effusive groups who have planned elaborate celebrations for the returning soul may suspend all their other activities. One subject of mine had this to say about his homecoming welcome:

> After my last life, my group organized one hell of a party with music, wine, dancing and singing. They arranged everything to look like a classical Roman festival with marble halls, togas and all the exotic furnishings prevalent in our many lives together in the ancient world. Melissa (a primary soulmate) was waiting for me right up front, re-creating the age that I remember her best and looking as radiant as ever.

Soul groups range between three and twenty-five members, with the average having about fifteen. There are times when souls from nearby cluster groups may want to connect with each other. Often this activity involves older souls who have made many friends from other groups with whom they have been associated over hundreds of past lives. . . .

Thus, homecoming can take place in two types of settings. A few souls might briefly meet a returning soul at the gateway and then leave in favor of a guide who takes them through some preliminary orientation. More commonly, the welcoming committee waits until the soul actually returns to their spirit group. This group may be isolated in a classroom, gathered around the steps of a temple, sitting in a garden, or the returning soul could encounter many groups in a study hall atmosphere. Souls who pass by other clusters on the way to their own berth often remark that other souls with whom they have been associated in past lives will look up and acknowledge their return with a smile or wave.

How a subject views their group cluster setting is based upon the soul's state of advancement, although memories of a schoolroom atmosphere are always very clear. In the spirit world, educational placement depends on the level of soul development. Simply because a soul has been incarnating on Earth since the Stone Age is no guarantee of high attainment. In my lectures I often remark about a client who took 4,000 years of past lives finally to conquer jealousy. I can report he is not a jealous person today, yet he has made little progress with fighting his own intolerance. It takes some students longer to get through certain lessons, just as in earthly classrooms. On the other hand, all highly advanced souls are old souls in terms of both knowledge and experience. . . .

Generally, the composition of a group of souls is made up of beings at about the same level of advancement, although they have their individual strengths and shortcomings. These attributes give the group balance. Souls assist one another with the cognitive aspects of absorbing information from life experiences as well as reviewing the way they handled

the feelings and emotions of their host bodies directly related to those experiences. Every aspect of a life is dissected,
even to the extent of reverse role playing in the group, to
bring greater awareness. By the time souls reach the intermediate levels they begin to specialize in those major areas
of interest where certain skills have been demonstrated. . . .

Energy Colors

One very meaningful aspect of my research has been the discovery of energy colors displayed by souls in the spirit world.
These colors relate to a soul's state of advancement. This information, gathered slowly over many years, has been one
indicator of progress during client assessments and also
serves to identify other souls my subjects see around them
while in a trance state. I found that typically, pure white de-
notes a younger soul and with advancement soul energy becomes more dense, moving into orange, yellow, green and finally the blue ranges. In addition to these center core auras,
there are subtle mixtures of halo colors within every group
that relate to the character aspects of each soul.

For want of a better system, I have classified soul development as moving from a level I beginner through various
learning stages to that of a master at level VI. These greatly
advanced souls are seen as having a deep indigo color. I have
no doubt even higher levels exist, but my knowledge of them
is restricted because I only receive reports from people who
are still incarnating. Frankly, I am not fond of the term
"level" to identify soul placement because this label clouds
the diversity of development attained by souls at any particular stage. Despite these misgivings, it is my subjects who use
"level" to describe where they are on the ladder of learning.
They are also quite modest about accomplishments. Regard-
less of my assessment, no client is inclined to state they are
an advanced soul. Once out of hypnosis, with a fully con-

scious self-gratifying mind in control, they are less reticent. While in a superconscious state during deep hypnosis, my subjects tell me that in the spirit world no soul is looked down upon as having less value than any other soul. We are all in a process of transformation to something greater than our current state of enlightenment. Each of us is considered uniquely qualified to make some contribution toward the whole, no matter how hard we are struggling with our lessons. If this were not true we would not have been created in the first place.

Levels of Soul Advancement

In my discussions of colors of advancement, levels of development, classrooms, teachers and students it would be easy to assume the ambiance of the spirit world is one of hierarchy. This conclusion would be quite wrong, according to all my clients. If anything, the spirit world is hierarchical in mental awareness. We tend to think of organizational authority on Earth as represented by power struggles, turf wars and the controlling use of a rigid set of rules within structure. There certainly is structure in the spirit world, but it exists within a sublime matrix of compassion, harmony, ethics and morality far beyond what we practice on Earth. In my experience the spirit world also has a far-reaching centralized personnel department for soul assignments. Yet there is a value system here of overwhelming kindness, tolerance, patience and absolute love. When reporting to me about such things, my subjects are humbled by the process.

I have an old college friend in Tucson who is an iconoclast and has resisted authority all his life, which is an attitude I can empathize with myself. My friend suspects the souls of my clients have been "brain washed" into believing they have control over their destiny. He believes authority of any kind—even spiritual authority—cannot exist without corruption and the abuse of privilege. My research reveals too much order upstairs, which is not to his liking.

Nevertheless, all my subjects believe they have had a multitude of choices in their past and that this will continue into the future. Advancement through the taking of personal responsibility does not involve dominance or status ranking but rather a recognition of potential. They see integrity and personal freedom everywhere in their life between lives.

A Soul's Free Will

In the spirit world we are not forced to reincarnate or participate in group projects. If souls want solitude they can have it. If they don't want to advance in their assignments, this too is honored. One subject told me, "I have skated through many easy lives and I like it that way because I haven't really wanted to work hard. Now that's going to change. My guide says, 'we are ready when you are.'" In fact, there is so much free will that if we are not ready to leave Earth's astral plane after death, for a variety of personal reasons, our guides will allow us to stay around until such time as we are prepared to go home. . . .

We have many choices both in and out of the spirit world. What is very evident to me about these choices is the intense desire of most souls to prove themselves worthy of the trust placed in them. We are expected to make mistakes in this process. The effort of moving toward a greater goodness and a conjunction with the Source that created us is the prime motivator of souls. Souls have feelings of humility at having been given the opportunity to incarnate in physical form.

The Existence of God

I have been asked many times if my subjects see the Source of Creation during their sessions. In my introduction I said

I could go only so far upriver toward the Source because of the limitations of working with people who are still incarnating. Advanced subjects talk about the time of conjunction when they will join the "Most Sacred Ones." In this sphere of dense purple light there is an all-knowing Presence. What all this means I cannot say, but I do know a Presence is felt when we go before our council of Elders. Once or twice between lives we visit this group of higher beings who are a step or two above our teacher-guides. In my first book, I gave a couple of case examples of these meetings. . . . I will go into greater detail about our visitations with these masters who are as close as I can come to the Creator. This is because it is here where an even higher source of divine knowledge is experienced by the soul. My clients call this energy force "the Presence."

The council is not a tribunal of judges nor a courtroom where souls appear to be tried and sentenced for wrongdoing, although I must admit that once in a while someone will tell me they feel going in front of the council is like being sent to the principal's office in school. Members of the council want to talk to us about our mistakes and what we can do to correct negative behavior in the next life.

This is the place where considerations for the right body in our next life begin. As the time approaches for rebirth, we go to a space where a number of bodies are reviewed that might meet our goals. We have a chance to look into the future here and actually test out different bodies before making a choice. Souls voluntarily select less than perfect bodies and difficult lives to address karmic debts or to work on different aspects of a lesson they have had trouble with in the past. Most souls accept the bodies offered to them in the selection room but a soul can reject what is offered and even delay reincarnating. Then, too, a soul might ask to go to a physical planet other than Earth for awhile. If we accept the new assignment, we are often sent to a preparation class to remind us of certain signposts and clues in the life to come, especially at those moments when primary soulmates come into our lives.

Finding a New Host

Finally, when the time comes for our return, we say a temporary goodbye to our friends and are escorted to the space of embarkation for the trip to Earth. Souls join their assigned hosts in the womb of the baby's mother sometime after the third month of pregnancy so they will have a sufficiently evolved brain to work with before term. As part of the fetal state they are still able to think as immortal souls while they get used to brain circuitry and the alter ego of their host. After birth, an amnesiac memory block sets in and souls meld their immortal character with the temporary human mind to produce a combination of traits for a new personality.

I use a systematic approach to reach the soul mind by employing a series of exercises for people in the early stages of hypnotic regression. This procedure is designed to gradually sharpen my subject's memories of their past and prepare them to analyze critically the images they will see of life in the spirit world. After the usual intake interview, I place the client in hypnosis very quickly. It is the deepening that is my secret. Over long periods of experimentation, I have come to realize that having a client in the normal alpha state of hypnosis is not adequate enough to reach the superconscious state of the soul mind. For this I must take the subject into the deeper theta ranges of hypnosis.

In terms of methodology, I may spend up to an hour with long visualizations of forest or seashore images, then I take the subject into their childhood years. I ask detailed questions about such things as the furniture in their house at age twelve, their favorite article of clothing at age ten, the toy they loved most at age seven and their earliest memories as a child between ages three and two. We do all this before I take the client down into their mother's womb for more questions and then into the most immediate past life for a short review. By the time the client has passed through the death scene of that life and reached the gateway to the spirit world, my bridge is complete. Continual hypnosis, deepening over the first hour, enhances the subject's disengagement from their earthly environment. They have also been conditioned to respond in detail to an intensive question and answer interview of their spiritual life. This will take us another two hours.

Subjects who come out of trance after mentally returning home have a look of awe on their faces that is far more profound than if they had just experienced a straight past life regression. For example, a client told me, "The spirit has a diversity and complex fluid quality beyond my ability adequately to interpret." Many former clients write me about how viewing their immortality changed their lives. Here is a sample of one letter:

> I have gained an indescribable sense of joy and freedom from learning my true identity. The amazing thing is that this knowledge was in my mind all the time. Seeing my non-judgmental master teachers left me in a glowing state. The insight that came to me was that the only thing of true importance in this material life is the way we live and how we treat other people. The circumstances of our life mean nothing compared to our compassion and acceptance of others. I now have a knowing rather than a feeling about why I am here and where I am going after death.

. . . There are many doorways to the truth. My truths come from a cumulation of great wisdom from multitudes of people who have graced my life as clients over many years.

Chapter 2

Fact or Fiction?

Evidence Against
Life After Death

Near-Death Experiences Are Not Proof of Life After Death

Susan Blackmore

According to the Gallup organization and near-death research studies, an estimated 13 million adults in the United States have had a near-death experience (NDE). Most experiencers agree that it had a profound effect on their life. However, whether these experiences actually prove the existence of an afterlife remains debatable. Susan Blackmore holds a Ph.D. in parapsychology from the University of Surrey, is the author of *The Meme Machine*, and is a respected expert in this field. She has studied NDEs for many years. Throughout her career she has written or been part of over forty books about NDEs, including *Dying to Live*. In the following article, Blackmore argues that NDEs are not proof of a life after death. She offers scientific explanations for all aspects of NDEs.

Susan Blackmore, "Near-Death Experiences: In or Out of the Body?" *Skeptical Inquirer*, vol. 16, 1991, pp. 34–35. Copyright © 1991 by *Skeptical Inquirer*. Reproduced by permission.

W hat is it like to die? Although most of us fear death to a greater or lesser extent, there are now more and more people who have "come back" from states close to death and have told stories of usually very pleasant and even joyful experiences at death's door.

For many experiencers, their adventures seem unquestionably to provide evidence for life after death, and the profound effects the experience can have on them is just added confirmation. By contrast, for many scientists these experiences are just hallucinations produced by the dying brain and of no more interest than an especially vivid dream.

So which is right? Are near-death experiences (NDEs) the prelude to our life after death or the very last experience we have before oblivion? I shall argue that neither is quite right: NDEs provide no evidence for life after death, and we can best understand them by looking at neurochemistry, physiology, and psychology; but they are much more interesting than any dream. They seem completely real and can transform people's lives. Any satisfactory theory has to understand that too—and that leads us to questions about minds, selves, and the nature of consciousness.

Deathbed Experiences

Toward the end of the [nineteenth] century the physical sciences and the new theory of evolution were making great progress, but many people felt that science was forcing out the traditional ideas of the spirit and soul. Spiritualism began to flourish, and people flocked to mediums to get in contact with their dead friends and relatives "on the other side." Spiritualists claimed, and indeed still claim, to have found proof of survival.

In 1882, the Society for Psychical Research was founded, and serious research on the phenomena began; but convincing evidence for survival is still lacking over one hundred years later. In 1926, a psychical researcher and Fellow of the Royal Society, Sir William Barrett, published a little book on deathbed visions. The dying apparently saw other worlds before they died and even saw and spoke to the dead. There were cases of music heard at the time of death and reports of attendants actually seeing the spirit leave the body.

With modern medical techniques, deathbed visions like these have become far less common. In those days people died at home with little or no medication and surrounded by their family and friends. Today most people die in the hospital and all too often alone. Paradoxically it is also improved medicine that has led to an increase in quite a different kind of report—that of the near-death experience. . . .

Explanations of the NDE and Astral Projection

Astral Projection and the Next World: Could we have another body that is the vehicle of consciousness and leaves the physical body at death to go on to another world? This, essentially, is the doctrine of astral projection. In various forms it is very popular and appears in a great deal of New Age and occult literature.

One reason may be that out-of-body experiences (OBEs) are quite common, quite apart from their role in NDEs. Surveys have shown that anywhere from 8 percent (in Iceland) to as much as 50 percent (in special groups, such as marijuana users) have had OBEs at some time during their lives. In my own survey of residents of Bristol [England] I found 12 percent. Typically these people had been resting or lying down and suddenly felt they had left their bodies, usually for no more than a minute or two.

A survey of more than 50 different cultures showed that almost all of them believe in a spirit or soul that could leave the body. So both the OBE and the belief in another body are common, but what does this mean? Is it just that we cannot bring ourselves to believe that we are nothing more than a mortal body and that death is the end? Or is there really another body? . . .

Testing the Theory of Astral Projection

The theory of astral projection is, at least in some forms, testable. In the earliest experiments mediums claimed they were able to project their astral bodies to distant rooms and see what was happening. They claimed not to taste bitter aloes on their real tongues, but immediately screwed up their faces in disgust when the substance was placed on their (invisible) astral tongues. Unfortunately these experiments were not properly controlled.

In other experiments, dying people were weighed to try to detect the astral body as it left. Early [in the twentieth] century a weight of about one ounce was claimed, but as the apparatus became more sensitive the weight dropped, implying that it was not a real effect. More recent experiments have used sophisticated detectors of ultraviolet and infrared, magnetic flux or field strength, temperature, or weight to try to capture the astral body of someone having an out-of-body experience. They have even used animals and human "detectors," but no one has yet succeeded in detecting anything reliably.

If something really leaves the body in OBEs, then you might expect it to be able to see at a distance, in other words to have extrasensory perception (ESP). There have been several experiments with concealed targets. One success was [a] subject . . . who lay on a bed with a five-digit number on a shelf above it. During the night she had an OBE and correctly reported the number, but critics argued that she could have climbed out of the bed to look. Apart from this one, the experiments tend, like so many in parapsychology, to provide equivocal results and no clear signs of any ESP.

So, this theory has been tested but seems to have failed its tests. If there really were astral bodies I would have expected us to have found something out about them by now—other than how hard it is to track them down!

In addition there are major theoretical objections to the idea of astral bodies. If you imagine that the person has gone to another world, perhaps along some "real" tunnel, then you have to ask what relationship there is between this world and the other one. If the other world is an extension of the physical, then it ought to be observable and measurable. The astral body, astral world, and tunnel ought to be detectable in some way, and we ought to be able to say where exactly the tunnel is going. The fact that we can't, leads many people to say the astral world is "on another plane," at a "higher level of vibration," and the like. But unless you can specify just what these mean the ideas are completely empty, even though they may sound appealing. Of course we can never prove that astral bodies don't exist, but my guess is that they probably don't and that this theory is not a useful way to understand OBEs.

Birth and the NDE

Another popular theory makes dying analogous with being born: that the out-of-body experience is literally just that—reliving the moment when you emerged from your mother's body. The tunnel is the birth canal and the white light is the light of the world into which you were born. Even the being of light can be "explained" as an attendant at the birth.

This theory was proposed by Stanislav Grof and Joan Halifax (1977) and popularized by the astronomer Carl Sagan (1979), but it is pitifully inadequate to explain the

NDE. For a start the newborn infant would not see anything like a tunnel as it was being born. The birth canal is stretched and compressed and the baby usually forced through it with the top of its head, not with its eyes (which are closed anyway) pointing forward. Also it does not have the mental skills to recognize the people around, and these capacities change so much during growing that adults cannot reconstruct what it was like to be an infant.

"Hypnotic regression to past lives" is another popular claim. In fact much research shows that people who have been hypnotically regressed give the appearance of acting like a baby or a child, but it is no more than acting. For example, they don't make drawings like a real five-year-old would do but like an adult imagines children do. Their vocabulary is too large and in general they overestimate the abilities of children at any given age. There is no evidence (even if the idea made sense) of their "really" going back in time.

Of course the most important question is whether this theory could be tested, and to some extent it can. For example, it predicts that people born by Caesarean section should not have the same tunnel experiences and OBEs. I conducted a survey of people born normally and those born by Caesarean (190 and 36 people, respectively). Almost exactly equal percentages of both groups had had tunnel experiences (36 percent) and OBEs (29 percent). I have not compared the type of birth of people coming close to death, but this would provide further evidence. . . .

Just Hallucinations

Perhaps we should give up and conclude that all the experiences are "just imagination" or "nothing but hallucinations." However, this is the weakest theory of all. The experiences must, in some sense, be hallucinations, but this is not, on its own, any explanation. We have to ask why are they these kinds of hallucinations? Why tunnels?

Some say the tunnel is a symbolic representation of the gateway to another world. But then why always a tunnel and not, say, a gate, doorway, or even the great River Styx? Why the light at the end of the tunnel? And why always above the body, not below it? I have no objection to the theory that the experiences are hallucinations. I only object to the idea that you can explain them by saying, "They are just hallucinations." This explains nothing. A viable theory would answer these questions without dismissing the experiences. That, even if only in tentative form, is what I shall try to provide.

The Physiology of the Tunnel

Tunnels do not only occur near death. They are also experienced in epilepsy and migraine, when falling asleep, meditating, or just relaxing, with pressure on both eyeballs, and with certain drugs, such as LSD, psilocybin, and mescaline. . . . It is as though the whole world becomes a rushing, roaring tunnel and you are flying along it toward a bright light at the end. No doubt many readers have also been there, for surveys show that about a third of people have—like this terrified man of 28 who had just had the anesthetic for a circumcision.

> I seemed to be hauled at "lightning speed" in a direct line tunnel into outer space; (not a floating sensation . . .) but like a rocket at a terrific speed. I appeared to have left my body.

In the 1930s, Heinrich Klüver, at the University of Chicago, noted four form constants in hallucinations: the tunnel, the spiral, the lattice or grating, and the cobweb. Their origin probably lies in the structure of the visual cortex, the part of the brain that processes visual information. Imagine that the outside world is mapped onto the back of the eye (on the retina), and then again in the cortex. The mathematics of this mapping (at least to a reasonable approximation) is well known.

Jack Cowan, a neurobiologist at the University of Chicago, has used this mapping to account for the tunnel. Brain activity is normally kept stable by some cells inhibiting others. Disinhibition (the reduction of this inhibitory activity) produces too much activity in the brain. This can occur near death (because of lack of oxygen) or with drugs like LSD, which interfere with inhibition. Cowan uses an analogy with fluid mechanics to argue that disinhibition will induce stripes of activity that move across the cortex. Using the mapping it can easily be shown that stripes in the cortex would appear like concentric rings or spirals in the visual world. In other words, if you have stripes in the cortex you will seem to see a tunnel-like pattern of spirals or rings.

This theory is important in showing how the structure of the brain could produce the same hallucination for everyone. However, I was dubious about the idea of these moving stripes, and also Cowan's theory doesn't readily explain the bright light at the center. So Tom Troscianko and I, at the University of Bristol, tried to develop a simpler theory. The most obvious thing about the representation in the cortex is that there are lots of cells representing the center of the visual field but very few for the edges. This means that you can see small things very clearly in the center, but if they are out at the edges you cannot. We took just this simple fact as a starting point and used a computer to simulate what would happen when you have gradually increasing electrical noise in the visual cortex.

The computer program starts with thinly spread dots of light, mapped in the same way as the cortex, with more toward the middle and very few at the edges. Gradually the number of dots increases, mimicking the increasing noise. Now the center begins to look like a white blob and the outer edges gradually get more and more dots. And so it expands until eventually the whole screen is filled with light. The appearance is just like a dark speckly tunnel with a white light at the end, and the light grows bigger and bigger (or nearer and nearer) until it fills the whole screen. . . .

If it seems odd that such a simple picture can give the impression that you are moving, consider two points. First, it is known that random movements in the periphery of the visual field are more likely to be interpreted by the brain as outward than inward movement. Second, the brain infers our own movement to a great extent from what we see. Therefore, presented with an apparently growing patch of flickering white light your brain will easily interpret it as yourself moving forward into a tunnel.

The theory also makes a prediction about NDEs in the blind. If they are blind because of problems in the eye but have a normal cortex, then they too should see tunnels. But if their blindness stems from a faulty or damaged cortex, they should not. These predictions have yet to be tested.

According to this kind of theory there is, of course, no real tunnel. Nevertheless there is a real physical cause of the tunnel experience. It is noise in the visual cortex. This way we can explain the origin of the tunnel without just dismissing the experiences and without needing to invent other bodies or other worlds.

Out-of-Body Experiences Explained

Like tunnels, OBEs are not confined to near death. They too can occur when just relaxing and falling asleep, with meditation, and in epilepsy and migraine. They can also, at least by a few people, be induced at will. . . .

It is important to remember that these experiences seem quite real. People don't describe them as dreams or fantasies but as events that actually happened. This is, I presume, why they seek explanations in terms of other bodies or other worlds.

However, we have seen how poorly the astral projection and birth theories cope with OBEs. What we need is a theory that involves no unmeasurable entities or untestable other worlds but explains why the experiences happen; and why they seem so real.

I would start by asking why anything seems real. You might think this is obvious—after all, the things we see out there are real aren't they? Well no, in a sense they aren't. As perceiving creatures all we know is what our senses tell us. And our senses tell us what is "out there" by constructing models of the world with ourselves in it. The whole of the world "out there" and our own bodies are really constructions of our minds. Yet we are sure, all the time, that this construction—if you like, this "model of reality"—is "real" while the other fleeting thoughts we have are unreal. We call the rest of them daydreams, imagination, fantasies, and so on. Our brains have no trouble distinguishing "reality" from "imagination." But this distinction is not given. It is one the brain has to make for itself by deciding which of its own models represents the world "out there." I suggest it does this by comparing all the models it has at any time and choosing the most stable one as "reality."

This will normally work very well. The model created by the senses is the best and most stable the system has. It is obviously "reality," while that image I have of the bar I'm going to go to later is unstable and brief. The choice is easy. By comparison, when you are almost asleep, very frightened, or nearly dying, the model from the senses will be confused and unstable. If you are under terrible stress or suffering oxygen deprivation, then the choice won't be so easy. All the models will be unstable.

So what will happen now? Possibly the tunnel being created by noise in the visual cortex will be the most stable model and so, according to my supposition, this will seem real. Fantasies and imagery might become more stable than the sensory model, and so seem real. The system will have lost input control.

OBEs and Memory

What then should a sensible biological system do to get back to normal? I would suggest that it could try to ask itself—as it were—"Where am I? What is happening?" Even a person under severe stress will have some memory left. They might recall the accident, or know that they were in hospital for an operation, or remember the pain of the heart attack. So they will try to reconstruct, from what little they can remember, what is happening.

Now we know something very interesting about memory models. Often they are constructed in a bird's-eye view. That is, the events or scenes are seen as though from above. If you find this strange, try to remember the last time . . . you walked along the seashore. Where are "you" looking from in this recalled scene? If you are looking from above you will see what I mean.

So my explanation of the OBE becomes clear. A memory model in bird's-eye view has taken over from the sensory model. It seems perfectly real because it is the best model the system has got at the time. Indeed, it seems real for just the same reason anything ever seems real.

This theory of the OBE leads to many testable predictions, for example, that people who habitually use bird's-eye views should be more likely to have OBEs. Both Harvey Irwin, an Australian psychologist, and myself have found that people who dream as though they were spectators have more OBEs, although there seems to be no difference for the waking use of different viewpoints. I have also found that people who can more easily switch viewpoints in their imagination are also more likely to report OBEs.

Of course this theory says that the OBE world is only a memory model. It should only match the real world when the person has already known about something or can deduce it from available information. This presents a big challenge for research on near death. Some researchers claim that people near death can actually see things that they couldn't possibly have known about. For example, the American cardiologist Michael Sabom claims that patients reported the exact behavior of needles on monitoring apparatus when they had their eyes closed and appeared to be unconscious. Further, he compared these descriptions with those of people imagining they were being resuscitated and found that the real patients gave far more accurate and detailed descriptions.

There are problems with this comparison. Most important, the people really being resuscitated could probably feel some of the manipulations being done on them and hear what was going on. Hearing is the last sense to be lost and, as you will realize if you ever listen to radio plays or news, you can imagine a very clear visual image when you can only hear something. So the dying person could build up a fairly accurate picture this way. Of course hearing doesn't allow you to see the behavior of needles, and so if Sabom is right I am wrong. We can only await further research to find out.

The Life Review

The experience of seeing excerpts from your life flash before you is not really as mysterious as it first seems. It has long been known that stimulation of cells in the temporal lobe of the brain can produce instant experiences that seem like the reliving of memories. Also, temporal-lobe epilepsy can produce similar experiences, and such seizures can involve other limbic structures in the brain, such as the amygdala and hippocampus, which are also associated with memory.

Imagine that the noise in the dying brain stimulates cells like this. The memories will be aroused and, according to my hypothesis, if they are the most stable model the system has at that time they will seem real. For the dying person they may well be more stable than the confused and noisy sensory model.

The link between temporal-lobe epilepsy and the NDE has formed the basis of a thorough neurobiological model of the NDE. They suggest that the brain stress consequent on the near-death episode leads to the release of neuropeptides and neurotransmitters (in particular the endogenous endorphins). These then stimulate the limbic system and other connected areas. In addition, the effect of the endorphins could account for the blissful and other positive emotional states so often associated with the NDE.

[Pediatrician Melvin] Morse provided evidence that some children deprived of oxygen treated with opiates did not have NDE-like hallucinations, and he and his colleagues have developed a theory based on the role of the neurotransmitter serotonin, rather than the endorphins. Research on the neurochemistry of the NDE is just beginning and should provide us with much more detailed understanding of the life review.

Of course there is more to the review than just memories. The person feels as though she or he is judging these life events, being shown their significance and meaning. But this too, I suggest, is not so very strange. When the normal world of the senses is gone and memories seem real, our perspective on our life changes. We can no longer be attached to our plans, hopes, ambitions, and fears, which fade away and become unimportant, while the past comes to life again. We can only accept it as it is, and there is no one to judge it but ourselves. This is, I think, why so many NDEers say they faced their past life with acceptance and equanimity.

Other Worlds

Now we come to what might seem the most extraordinary parts of the NDE: the worlds beyond the tunnel and OBE. But I think you can now see that they are not so extraordinary at all. In this state the outside world is no longer real, and inner worlds are. Whatever we can imagine clearly enough will seem real. And what will we imagine when we know we are dying? I am sure for many people it is the world they expect or hope to see. Their minds may turn to people they have known who have died before them or to the world they hope to enter next. Like the other images we have been considering, these will seem perfectly real.

Finally, there are those aspects of the NDE that are ineffable—they cannot be put into words. I suspect that this is because some people take yet another step, a step into nonbeing. I shall try to explain this by asking another question. What is consciousness? If you say it is a thing, another body, a substance, you will only get into the kinds of difficulty we got into with OBEs. I prefer to say that consciousness is just what it is like being a mental model. In other words, all the mental models in any person's mind are all conscious, but only one is a model of "me." This is the one that I think of as myself and to which I relate everything else. It gives a core to my life. It allows me to think that I am a person, something that lives on all the time. It allows me to ignore the fact that "I" change from moment to moment and even disappear every night in sleep.

Now when the brain comes close to death, this model of self may simply fall apart. Now there is no self. It is a strange and dramatic experience. For there is no longer an experiencer—yet there is experience.

This state is obviously hard to describe, for the "you" who is trying to describe it cannot imagine not being. Yet this profound experience leaves its mark. The self never seems quite the same again.

The After-Effects

I think we can now see why an essentially physiological event can change people's lives so profoundly. The experience has jolted their usual (and erroneous) view of the relationship between themselves and the world. We all too easily assume that we are some kind of persistent entity inhabiting a perishable body. But, as the Buddha taught we have to see through that illusion. The world is only a construction of an information-processing system, and the self is too. I believe that the NDE gives people a glimpse into the nature of their own minds that is hard to get any other way. Drugs can produce it temporarily, mystical experiences can do it for rare people, and long years of practice in meditation or mindfulness can do it. But the NDE can out of the blue strike anyone and show them what they never knew before, that their body is only that—a lump of flesh—that they are not so very important after all. And that is a very freeing and enlightening experience.

And Afterwards?

If my analysis of the NDE is correct, we can extrapolate to the next stage. Lack of oxygen first produces increased activity through disinhibition, but eventually it all stops. Since it is this activity that produces the mental models that give rise to consciousness, then all this will cease. There will be no more experience, no more self, and so that, as far as my constructed self is concerned, is the end.

Reincarnation Is Fiction

Hieromonk Seraphim Rose

Today more than ever, people are faced with an unending amount of spiritual choices. There is a religion and belief for every purpose. Christianity is still the most popular form of religion in the United States. However, many people combine their Christian beliefs with other religious beliefs. The spirit world is a controversial area to a lot of religious people. Issues such as ghosts, reincarnation, and entry into heaven are regular topics of debate.

The spiritual leader and cofounder of the Saint Herman of Alaska Brotherhood and monastery in Platina, California, Hieromonk Seraphim Rose, was a devoted Orthodox Christian. He spent seven years living in an eight-foot-by-twelve-foot shelter in the desert, praying, meditating, and writing. In the following essay Rose examines all sides of reincarnation from a Christian viewpoint and explains his belief that reincarnation is impossible.

Hieromonk Seraphim Rose, *The Soul After Death*. Platina, CA: Saint Herman of Alaska Brotherhood, 1982. Copyright © 1980 by Saint Herman of Alaska Brotherhood. Reproduced by permission.

Among the occult ideas which are now being widely discussed and sometimes accepted by those who have "out-of-
body" and "after-death" experiences, and even by some scientists, is the idea of reincarnation: that the soul after death
does not undergo the Particular Judgment and then dwell in
heaven or hell awaiting the resurrection of the body and the
Last Judgment, but (evidently after a longer or shorter stay
on the "astral plane") comes back to earth and occupies a
new body, whether of a beast or of another man.

This idea was widespread in pagan antiquity in the West,
before it was replaced by Christian ideas; but its spread today is largely owing to the influence of Hinduism and Buddhism, where it is commonly accepted. Today the idea is
usually "humanized," in that people assume their "previous
lives" were as men, whereas the more common idea both
among Hindus and Buddhists and among ancient Greeks
and Romans is that it is rather rare to achieve "incarnation"
as a man, and that most of today's "incarnations" are as
beasts, insects, and even plants.

Those who believe in this idea say that it accounts for all
of the many "injustices" of earthly life, as well as for seemingly unexplainable phobias: if one is born blind, or in conditions of poverty, it is as a just reward for one's actions in a
"previous life" (or, as Hindus and Buddhists say, because of
one's "bad karma"); if one is afraid of water, it is because
one drowned in a "previous existence."

Believers in reincarnation do not have any very thorough
philosophy of the origin and destination of the soul, nor
any convincing proofs to support their theory; its main at-
tractions are the superficial ones of seeming to provide "justice" on earth, of explaining some psychic mysteries, and of

providing some semblance of "immortality" for those who do not accept this on Christian grounds.

Reincarnation Does Not Explain Injustices

On deeper reflection, however, the theory of reincarnation offers no real explanation of injustices at all: if one suffers in this life for sins and mistakes in another lifetime which one cannot remember, and for which (if one was "previously" a beast) one cannot even be held responsible, and if (according to Buddhist teaching) there is even no "self" that survives from one "incarnation" to the next, and one's past mistakes were literally someone else's—then there is no recognizable justice at all, but only a blind suffering of evils whose origin is not to be traced out. The Christian teaching of the fall of Adam, which is the origin of all the world's evils, offers a much better explanation of injustices in the world; and the Christian revelation of God's perfect justice in His judgment of men for eternal life in heaven or hell renders unnecessary and trivial the idea of attaining "justice" through successive "incarnations" in this world.

In recent decades the idea of reincarnation has achieved a remarkable popularity in the Western world, and there have been numerous cases suggesting the "rememberance" of "past lives"; many people also return from "out-of-body" experiences believing that these experiences suggest or instill the idea of reincarnation. What are we to think of these cases?

Very few of these cases, it should be noted, offer "proof" that is any more than vaguely circumstantial, and could easily be the product of simple imagination: a child is born with a mark on his neck, and subsequently "remembers" that he was hanged as a horse thief in a "previous life"; a person fears heights, and then "remembers" that he died by falling in his "past life"; and the like. The natural human tendency of fantasy renders such cases useless as "proof" of reincarnation.

The Pitfalls of Regressive Hypnosis

In many cases, however, such "previous lives" have been discovered by a hypnotic technique known as "regressive hypnosis," which has in many cases given striking results in the recall of events long forgotten by the conscious mind, even as far back as infancy. The hypnotist brings a person "back" to infancy, and then asks: "What about *before that?*" Often, in such cases, a person will "remember" his "death" or even a whole different lifetime; what are we to think of such memories?

Well-trained hypnotists themselves will admit the pitfalls of "regressive hypnosis." Dr. Arthur C. Hastings, a California specialist in the psychology of communication, notes that "the most obvious thing that happens under hypnosis is that the person is extremely open to any subtle, unconscious, nonverbal, as well as verbal suggestions of the hypnotist and they are extremely compliant. If you ask them to go to a past life, and they don't *have* a past life, they will invent one for you! If you suggest that they saw a UFO, they would have seen a UFO. A Chicago-based hypnotist, Dr. Larry Garrett, who has done some 500 hypnotic regressions himself, notes that these regressions are often inaccurate even when it is only a matter of remembering a past event in *this* life: "A lot of times people fabricate things, from either wishful thinking, fantasies, dreams, things such as this. . . . Anyone who is into hypnosis and does any type of regression would find out that many times people have such a vivid imagination that they will sit there and make up all kinds of things just to please the hypnotist."

Another researcher on this question writes: "This method is fraught with hazards, chief of which is the unconscious mind's tendency toward dramatic fantasy. What comes out in hypnosis may be, in effect, a dream of the kind of previous existence the subject would like to have lived or believes, correctly or incorrectly, that he did live. . . . One psychologist instructed a number of hypnotized subjects to remember a previous existence, and they did, without exception. Some of these accounts were replete with colorful details and seemed convincing. . . . However, when the psychologist rehypnotized them they were able, in trance, to trace every element in the accounts of previous existence to some normal source—a person they had known in childhood, scenes from novels they had read or movies they had seen years before, and so on."

But what of those cases, publicized widely of late, when there is "objective proof" of one's "previous life"—when a person "remembers" details of time and places he could not possibly have known by himself, and which can be checked by historical documents?

Such cases seem very convincing to those already inclined to believe in reincarnation; but this kind of "proof" is not different from the standard information provided by the "spirits" at seances (which can also be of a very striking kind), and there is no reason to suppose that the source is different. If the "spirits" at seances are quite clearly demons, then the information on one's "previous lives" can also be supplied by demons. The aim in both cases is the same: to confuse men with a dazzling display of seemingly "supernatural" knowledge, and thus to deceive them concerning the true nature of life after death and leave them spiritually unprepared for it.

A Lack of Proof

Even occultists who are favorable in general to the idea of reincarnation admit that the "proof" for reincarnation can be interpreted in various ways. One American popularizer of occult ideas believes that "most reported instances giving evidence of reincarnation could possibly be cases of possession." "Possession," according to such occultists, occurs when a "dead" person takes possession of a living body and the latter's personality and very identity seem to change, thus causing the impression that one is being dominated by the characteristics of one's "previous life." Those beings that "possess" men, of course, are demons, no matter how much they may masquerade as the souls of the dead. The recent famous *Twenty Cases Suggestive of Reincarnation* by Dr. Ian Stevenson seems, indeed, to be a collection of cases of such "possession."

The early Christian Church fought the idea of reincarnation, which entered the Christian world through Eastern teachings such as those of the Manicheans. [Origen of Alexandria, a great early spiritual leader, performed] false teaching of the "pre-existence of souls" was closely related to these teachings, and at the Fifth Ecumenical Council in Constantinople in 553 it was strongly condemned and its followers anathematized. Many individual Fathers of the Church wrote against it, notably St. Ambrose of Milan in the West (*On Belief in the Resurrection*, Book II), St. Gregory of Nyssa in the East (*On the Soul and the Resurrection*), and others.

Three Basic Reasons That Refute Reincarnation

For the present-day Orthodox Christian who is tempted by this idea, or who wonders about the supposed "proof" of it, it is perhaps sufficient to reflect on three basic Christian dogmas which conclusively refute the very possibility of reincarnation:

1. *The resurrection of the body.* Christ rose from the dead in the very body which had died the death of all men, and became the first-fruits of all men, whose bodies will also be resurrected on the last day and rejoined to their souls in order to live eternally in heaven or hell, according to God's

just judgment of their life on earth. This resurrected body, like that of Christ Himself, will be different from our earthly bodies in that it will be more refined and more like the angelic nature, without which it could not dwell in the Heavenly Kingdom, where there is no death or corruption; but it will still be the *same body*, miraculously restored and made fit by God for eternal life, as Ezekiel saw in his vision of the "dry bones" (Ezek. 37:1–14). In heaven the redeemed will recognize each other. The body is thus an inalienable part of the whole person who will live forever, and the idea of many bodies belonging to the same person denies the very nature of the Heavenly Kingdom which God has prepared for those who love Him.

2. *Our redemption by Jesus Christ.* God took flesh and through His life, suffering, and death on the Cross redeemed us from the dominion of sin and death. Through His Church, we are saved and made fit for the Heavenly Kingdom, with no "penalty" to pay for our past transgressions. But according to the idea of reincarnation, if one is "saved" at all it is only after many lifetimes of working out the consequences of one's sins. This is the cold and dreary legalism of the pagan religions which was totally abolished by Christ's sacrifice on the Cross; the thief on His right hand received salvation in an instant through his faith in the Son of God, the "bad karma" of his evil deeds being obliterated by the grace of God.

3. *The Judgment. It is appointed unto men once to die, but after this the judgment* (Heb. 9:27). Human life is a single, definite period of trial, after which there is no "second chance," but only God's judgment (which is both just and merciful) of a man according to the state of his soul when this life is finished.

In these three doctrines the Christian revelation is quite precise and definite, in contrast to the pagan religions which do not believe either in the resurrection or in redemption, and are vague about judgment and the future life. The one answer to all supposed experiences or remembrances of "previous lives" is precisely the clear-cut teaching of Christianity about the nature of human life and God's dealings with men.

Life After Death Cannot Be Scientifically Proven

Paul Kurtz

As it is becoming increasingly popular to adopt New Age beliefs into traditional ways of thinking, it is also popular to believe what is read or talked about without evidence. The Committee for the Scientific Investigation of Claims of the Paranormal, or CSICOP, works at investigating paranormal claims, often debunking common beliefs. Paul Kurtz holds a Ph.D. in philosophy from Columbia University and is currently chairman of CSICOP. He has written more than thirty books and over six hundred articles, many on the subject of paranormal investigation. In the following article, Kurtz explains why he believes that there is no scientific proof of life after death.

Paul Kurtz, "The New Paranatural Paradigm: Claims of Communicating with the Dead," *Skeptical Inquirer*, vol. 24, November 2000, p. 27. Copyright © 2000 by *Skeptical Inquirer*. Reproduced by permission.

A new paranatural paradigm seems to be emerging in postmodern culture. There is great public fascination with a paranatural/paranormal conception of the universe, fed in large part by the mass media and encouraged by a number of "fringe sciences," which claim to support this outlook. The cultural backdrop for this is the development of post-modernism in the academy—the denial that science provides us with objective truth, the belief that it is only one mythic narrative among others, and that a New Age paradigm is emerging that displaces or drastically modifies scientific naturalism.

What do I mean by the term "paranatural"? Science presupposes naturalism; that is, it seeks to develop causal explanations of natural phenomena, and it tests its hypotheses and theories by reference to the principles of logic, empirical observation, experimental prediction, and confirmation.

This is in contrast with supernatural explanations, which claim to deal with an order of existence beyond the visible or observable universe, and attributes events to occult causes. Supernaturalism postulates divine powers intervening miraculously in natural causal sequences. Thus it is alleged that the natural and material universe needs to be supplemented by a supernatural reality, which transcends human understanding and can only be approached by mysticism and faith. The domain of faith, it is said, supplements the domain of reason.

There are, however, two classes of events that stand between the natural and supernatural realms and enable us in some sense to deal with the occult. These refer to (1) paranormal and (2) paranatural phenomena. The term "paranormal" was used in the past century by parapsychologists (such as J.B. Rhine and Samuel Soal) to refer to a class of anomalous events that its proponents claimed were inexplicable in terms of normal materialistic sciences. "Para" meant "besides, alongside of, or beyond" naturalistic psychology. Nonetheless, these parapsychologists maintain that it was possible to describe and perhaps interpret these events experimentally, and they did so by referring to a range of psi phenomena, which referred to ESP, telepathy, clairvoyance, precognition, and psychokinesis.

There is another range of events, which I have labeled as "paranatural," that deal with still other dimensions of reality: classical mystical or supernatural claims that allegedly intrude into our universe from without. I am here referring primarily to a theistic order of reality and to phenomena including discarnate souls, intelligent design, and "creation science." Visitations from extraterrestrials beyond this world may be considered to be both paranormal and paranatural. Included under this rubric of "paranatural" are some classical religious phenomena, such as weeping statues, stigmata, exorcism and possession, faith healing, the Shroud of Turin, past-life regressions used as evidence for reincarnation, historical revelations by prophets who carry messages from On High, and other so-called religious miracles. All of these have an empirical component and are not completely transcendental, and hence they are capable of some experimental testing and historical reconstruction of their claims. Although these anomalous events are beyond nature, in one sense, proponents of them seek to offer some kind of empirical evidence to support their hypotheses that there are nonnatural, nonmaterial, or spiritual processes at work in the universe.

I disagree with the claims of the defenders of the para: I do not think that either the paranormal or paranatural exist outside of nature or that they constitute dimensions of reality that undermine naturalism. Para is a substitute for our ignorance at any one time in history (as is the term "miracle," which is interjected when we do not understand the causes of phenomena). Indeed, as we expand the frontiers of knowledge, phenomena considered para can, I submit, be given naturalistic or normal explanations, and this range of phenomena can either be interpreted by the existing body of explanatory scientific principles or by the introduction of new ones.

The Paranatural Paradigm and Life After Death

I wish to illustrate this by dealing with the intriguing question: What is the evidence for life after death? Can we communicate with the dead? That is, Are we able to be in touch with people who have died? Do they have some form of existence, perhaps as "discarnate spirits" or "disembodied souls"? This is an age-old question that is related to faith in immortality and a very deep hunger for it. Although it has been interpreted as "paranormal," it may more appropriately be considered to be "paranatural" because of its religious significance. Indeed, for the great supernatural religions of the world—Christianity, Judaism, and Islam—belief in an afterlife and the promise of heaven are central.

At present there is intense popular interest in these questions in the United States. It is stimulated by the mass media, at least as measured by the number of popular books, magazine articles, movies, and television and radio programs devoted to the theme. The films *The Sixth Sense* (with Bruce Willis and Haley Osment) and *Frequency* are examples of the prevailing interest, as are the best-selling books by James Van Praagh (*Talking to Heaven*, 1997; *Reaching to Heaven*, 1999), John Edward (*One Last Time*, 1998), Sylvia Browne (*The Other Side and Back*, 1999), and Rosemary Altea (*You Own the Power*, 1999). Dan Rather on CBS, the Fox TV network, Larry King Live, and other talk-show hosts have devoted many uncritical programs to these claims. For example, the HBO TV network once did a special, "Life Afterlife," purporting to present the scientific examination of survival. It interviewed dozens of people, all of whom claim to have communicated with the dead, and several parapsychologists, all arguing the case for survival. Included in this special were critical comments by two skeptics—one more than usual! This is supposed to constitute a "balanced" documentary, and it is typical of the state of American media when dealing with paranatural or paranormal claims. There are all too few objective programs examining such questions; most favor a spiritual-paranormal interpretation. . . .

A History of Life After Death Claims

. . . Science has been investigating our ability to communicate with the dead for at least 150 years, and it has attempted to discover empirical evidence in support of the claim. It began to do so with the emergence of spiritualism in the nineteenth century; more specifically, with the Fox sisters (Margaret and Kate), two young girls in Hydesville, New York (outside of Rochester), who in 1848 first claimed that they could receive messages from "the spirit world beyond." In their presence, there were strange rappings; people would receive answers to their questions spelled out by the number of taps (Kurtz 1985). The basic premise was that human personality survived death and could communicate with specially endowed mediums. In the late nineteenth century and early twentieth century spiritualism swept the United States, England, and Europe. Thousands of mediums soon appeared, all seemingly capable of communicating with the dead. The most popular method of investigation was to try to communicate in a specially darkened seance room, wherein the discarnate entity would make its presence known by physical or verbal manifestations: table tipping, levitation of objects, ectoplasmic emissions, tele-portation, materializations, automatic writings, etc.

A committee of medical doctors at the University of Buffalo tested the Fox sisters in 1851 and attributed their raps to the cracking of their toe knuckles or knee caps against a wooden floor or bedstead. The physicians did a controlled experiment by placing the girls' feet on pillows, and nothing happened. The great physicist Michael Farraday investigated table tipping (1852) and found that it was due to pressure exerted by the fingers of the sitters (whether voluntarily or involuntarily). Sir Walter Crookes investigated the most colorful mediums of the day, D.D. Home (1871) and Florence Cook (1873), and thought that they had special abilities of mediumship—though critics believe that he was duped by both (Hall 1962, 1984).

The Society for Psychical Research was founded in 1882 in Great Britain by Henry Sidgwick, Richard Hodgson, F.W.H. Myers, Edmund Gurney, and others to investigate survival of life after death, among other questions. The American branch of the Society for Psychical Research was founded in 1885 by William James at Harvard. These researchers examined reports of apparitions and ghostly hauntings. It was difficult to corroborate these subjective eyewitness accounts and so these investigations focused on physical manifestations. There were numerous photographs of ghosts—which it was soon discovered could easily be doctored. Many famous mediums such as Eusapia Palladino (in Italy) and Leonora Piper (in Boston) were tested under controlled conditions in an effort to determine whether they possessed extraordinary powers.

Palladino was especially elusive, and the scientific community was split as to whether she was fraudulent. The Feilding Report was an account of sittings done in Naples (1909) by a team of scientists who thought she was genuine. Palladino was also tested in the United States at Harvard by Hugo Muensterberg (1909) and at Columbia University (1910) by a team of scientists; and in both cases the physical levitation of the table behind her and the feeling of being pinched by her spirit control (called John King) was found to be caused by her adroit ability to stretch her leg in contortions and to pinch sitters with her toes, or levitate a small table behind her. This was detected by having a man dressed in black crawl under the table and see her at work. A subsequent Feilding report (1911) also found that she had cheated (Kurtz 1985).

Late in his career the famous magician Houdini (1874–1926) exposed several bogus mediums. By the 1920s the spiritualist movement was thoroughly discredited, because when the controls were tightened, the effect disappeared; skeptics insisted that if a person claims to be in contact with a spiritual entity, there must be some independent physical corroboration by impartial observers (Houdini 1924, 1981).

In the 1930s the survival question in science was laid aside. J.B. Rhine and others focused instead on psi phenomena, again with controversial results, because scientists demanded replicable experiments by neutral observers, which were difficult to come by (Hansel 1980). In any case, whether or not psi existed was independent of the survival question.

Spiritualism Returns

In recent decades interest in the survival question has reappeared. This is rather surprising to skeptical investigators. No doubt this revival of interest is due in part to the growth of religiosity and spirituality on the broader American cultural scene, but is also due to the sensationalism of the mass media. I can only briefly outline some of the claims that had been made and the kinds of research that has been done. Most of this work is highly questionable, for the standards of rigorous methodological inquiry so essential to science seem to have declined drastically from what occurred in the early part of the last century.

(1) Channeling to the other side. Surprisingly, a new class of mediums, now called channelers, have emerged (such as James Van Praagh, John Edward, Sylvia Browne, and Rosemary Altea previously cited) who claim to be able to put themselves into immediate contact with a dead relative or friend and to convey a message back from them. Thus, what we have are subjective reports based on the word of the channeler that he or she is in touch with the departed spirit. There are two ways that this is done. First, there are "hot" readings, when the channeler may know something by previous research about the person being read. A good case of this is Arthur Ford, who did a reading of Bishop James Pike and claimed he was in contact with his son who had committed suicide. It was discovered after Ford's death that he had done extensive background investigation of Pike's son before the reading. The most common method used, however, is the skillful use of "cold readings" by the channeler. The public here is taken in by flim-flammery, and there is all too little effort to critically examine the claims made.

There has been a massive shift in the methodology used. If in previous decades scientists demanded some corroborative and/or physical manifestation of mediumship, today all rigorous standards of evidence and verification seem to have been abandoned. Psychologist Ray Hyman has shown how a psychic gives a general cold reading: if he throws out messages from the spirit world to an audience someone will usually emerge to whom it fits (Hyman 1977). Thus, he may ask, "Does anyone know a Mary, or a William?" And most likely a person will step forth who does, and then the reading proceeds, on a hit-and-miss basis. The skillful channeler simply has to have one or two lucky hits to mystify the audience.

(2) Apparitions and other sightings. Similar considerations apply to the epidemic of eyewitness testimonials that people have been reporting of ghostly apparitions, angels, and other ethereal entities. Such stories are pervasive today, since a tale once uttered may spread rapidly throughout the population; this is facilitated by the mass media and becomes contagious. If someone claims to see ghosts or angels, other people, perhaps millions, may likewise begin to encounter them.

What is so curious is that people who see ghosts usually see them clothed. It is one thing to say that a discarnate soul has survived, but that his or her clothing and other physical objects have survived is both amusing and contrary to the laws of physics.

The most parsimonious explanation that we have for this phenomenon is that it is in the eye of the beholder, satisfying some deep-felt need, a transcendental temptation or will-to-believe. The demand for independent objective verification seems to be ignored. It is puzzling why so many people will accept uncorroborated subjective reports, particularly when we find them unreliable. The death of a loved one can cause untold psychological trauma, and there are powerful motives, psychological and indeed sociological, for believing in their survival. Thus there are naturalistic psychological and sociological explanations that better account for the prevalence of such phenomenological givens, without the need to postulate discarnate beings or our ability to communicate with them.

Let me briefly outline two other areas of survival research, which at least claim to be more carefully designed.

(3) Death-bed visions. Osis and Haraldsson (1974, 1977) sent out questionnaires to doctors and nurses to ask them to describe the verbal accounts of death-bed visions of people in their last moments of dying. The question is whether these persons were able to communicate with departed friends or relatives at the last moment or were merely hallucinating, as skeptics suggest they were. In any case, virtually all of this data is second-hand, and is influenced by cultural expectations that when we die we will meet people on the other side.

(4) The phenomenology of near-death experience. This is a very popular area of research today, widely touted as evidence for communication, and based on first-hand testimony. Much research has gone into this intriguing area by Raymond Moody (1975, 1977), Elizabeth Kubler-Ross (1981), Kenneth Ring (1980, 1984, 1998), Michael Sabom (1982), and Melvin Morse (1990), among others. These extended phenomenological reports claim to give us evidence from the other side from people who were dying and resuscitated. There is an out-of-body experience, a vision of a tunnel, a bright light, a recall of one's life, and perhaps a meeting of beings on the other side.

Critics claim that the descriptive collage offered is of the dying process, and that in no case do we have reports of persons who have died (i.e., experienced brain death) and communicated with those on the other side. There are a variety of alternative naturalistic explanations. Skeptics maintain we are most likely dealing with psychological phenomena, where the person facing death has either hallucinations, has reached a state of depersonalization, and/or there are changes in brain chemistry and the nervous system (Blackmore 1993). Some have postulated that the discarnate entities or divine beings encountered on the other side are colored by the socio-cultural context (Kellehear 1996); though proponents maintain that in spite of this there is a common core of similarities. Some have said that falls or accidents where a person thinks he is about to die, but survives, can cause analogous out-of-body experiences and

panoramic reviews (Russell Noyes 1972, 1977). Not everyone who is dying reports near-death experiences; many
people who are not dying report having them. Sleep paral-
ysis and hypnopompic and hypnagogic dream states are factors in common out-of-body experiences. Ronald Siegel
(1981) maintains that similar NDEs can be induced by hal-
lucinogens. Karl Jansen (1996) has presented evidence that
they can be stimulated by the dissociative drug ketamine.
Various conditions can precipitate an NDE, such as low
blood sugar, oxygen deprivation, reduced blood flow,
temporal-lobe epilepsy, etc., and can lead to an altered state
of consciousness. For skeptics, in no case can we say that the
person has died and returns; what we are dealing with is the
process or belief that one is dying.

Analytic philosophers have pointed out additional serious conceptual difficulties in the hypothesis that nonphysical beings are communicating with us—there is a sharp
mind/body dualism here. Perhaps the real question is not
whether there is sufficient evidence for "x," but the meaning
of "x"; and whether we can communicate with "disembodied entities" who have a level of consciousness without sensory organs or a brain. Some have claimed that the communication is "telepathic," but the experimental evidence
for telepathy is itself questionable.

Conclusion

After a quarter of a century in this field of research, I find
that eyewitness testimony is notoriously unreliable, and
that unless carefully controlled studies and standards are
applied, people can deceive themselves and others into believing that almost anything is true and real—from past-life
regression and extraterrestrial abductions to satanic infesta-
tions and near-death experiences.

What should be the posture of the scientific investigator

about paranatural survival claims? Clearly, we need an open mind, and we should not reject a priori any such claim; if claims are responsibly framed they should be carefully evaluated. After a century and a half of scientific research, what are we to conclude? I submit that there is insufficient reliable or objective evidence that some individuals are able to reach another plane of existence beyond this world and/or communicate with the dead. As far as we know, the death of the body entails the death of psychological functions, consciousness, and/or the personality; and there is no reason to believe that ghosts hover and haunt and/or can communicate with us.

I realize that this flies in the face of what the preponderance of humans wish to believe, but science should deal as best it can with what is the case, not with what we would like it to be. Unfortunately, scientific objectivity today has an uphill battle in this area in the face of media hype and the enormous public fascination with paranormal and paranatural claims.

Psychics Do Not Prove Life After Death

Joe Nickell

Losing a loved one is often difficult. Many people turn to psychic mediums to contact their dead relatives to reassure themselves and make final contact. Critics argue that psychics take advantage of the grieving. Joe Nickell is a paranormal investigator who believes psychics are frauds. In the following article he exposes a popular psychic's onstage act and explains the different techniques employed by him, including the art of cold and hot readings. Nickell believes such fraud is proof that psychics cannot contact the dead.

Superstar "psychic medium" John Edward is a stand-up guy. Unlike the spiritualists of yore, who typically plied their trade in dark-room séances, Edward and his ilk often perform before live audiences and even under the glare of

Joe Nickell, "John Edward: Hustling the Bereaved," *Skeptical Inquirer*, November/December 2001. Copyright © 2001 by *Skeptical Inquirer*. Reproduced by permission.

TV lights. Indeed, Edward (a pseudonym: he was born John MaGee Jr.) has his own popular show on the SciFi channel called *Crossing Over*, which has gone into national syndication. I was asked by television newsmagazine *Dateline NBC* to study Edward's act: was he really talking to the dead? . . .

I have investigated various mediums, sometimes attending séances undercover and once obtaining police warrants against a fraudulent medium from the notorious Camp Chesterfield spiritualist center in Indiana. The camp is the subject of the book *The Psychic Mafia*, written by a former medium who recanted and revealed the tricks of floating trumpets (with disembodied voices), ghostly apparitions, materializing "apports," and other fake phenomena—some of which I have also witnessed firsthand.

Mental Mediumship

The new breed of spiritualists—like Edward, James Van Praagh, Rosemary Altea, Sylvia Browne, and George Anderson—avoid the physical approach with its risks of exposure and possible criminal charges. Instead they opt for the comparatively safe "mental mediumship" which involves the purported use of psychic ability to obtain messages from the spirit realm.

This is not a new approach, since mediums have long done readings for their credulous clients. In the early days they exhibited "the classic form of trance mediumship, as practiced by shamans and oracles," giving spoken "'spirit messages' that ranged all the way from personal (and sometimes strikingly accurate) trivia to hours-long public trance-lectures on subjects of the deepest philosophical and religious import."

Some mediums produced "automatic" or "trance" or "spirit" writing, which the entities supposedly dictated to the medium or produced by guiding his or her hand. Such writings could be in flowery language indeed, as in this excerpt from one spirit writing in my collection:

> Oh my Brother—I am so glad to be able to come here with you and hold sweet communion for it has been a long time since I have controlled this medium but I remember how well used I had become to her magnetism[,] but we will soon get accustomed to her again and then renew the pleasant times we used to have. I want to assure you that we are all here with you this afternoon[—]Father [,] Mother[,] little Alice[—]and so glad to find it so well with you and we hope and feel dear Brother that you have seen the darkest part of life and that times are not with you now as they have been. . . .

and so on in this talkative fashion. . . .

Problems with Cold Readings

By contrast, today's spirits—whom John Edward and his fellow mediums supposedly contact—seem to have poor memories and difficulty communicating. For example, in one of his on-air séances (on *Larry King Live*, June 19, 1998), Edward said: "I feel like there's a J- or G-sounding name attached to this." He also perceived "Linda or Lindy or Leslie; who's this L name?" Again, he got a "Maggie or Margie, or some M-G-sounding name," and yet again heard from "either Ellen or Helen, or Eleanore—it's like an Ellen-sounding name." Gone is the clear-speaking eloquence of yore; the dead now seem to mumble.

The spirits also seemingly communicate to Edward et al. as if they were engaging in pantomime. As Edward said of one alleged spirit communicant, in a *Dateline*, "He's pointing to his head; something had to affect the mind or the head, from what he's showing me." No longer, apparently, can the dead speak in flowing Victorian sentences, but instead are reduced to gestures, as if playing a game of charades.

One suspects, of course, that it is not the imagined spirits who have changed but rather the approach today's mediums have chosen to employ. It is, indeed, a shrewd technique known as "cold reading"—so named because the subject walks in "cold"; that is, the medium lacks advance information about the person. It is an artful method of gleaning information from the sitter, then feeding it back as mystical revelation.

The "psychic" can obtain clues by observing dress and body language (noting expressions that indicate when one is on or off track), asking questions (which if correct will appear as "hits" but otherwise will seem innocent queries), and inviting the subject to interpret the vague statements offered. For example, nearly anyone can respond to the mention of a common object (like a ring or watch) with a personal recollection that can seem to transform the mention into a hit.

It should not be surprising that Edward is skilled at cold reading, an old fortunetelling technique. His mother was a "psychic junkie" who threw fortunetelling "house parties," one of the alleged clairvoyants advising the then-fifteen-year-old that he had "wonderful psychic abilities." He began doing card readings for friends and family, then progressed to psychic fairs where he soon learned that names and other "validating information" sometimes applied to the dead rather than the living. Eventually he changed his billing from "psychic" to "psychic medium." The revised approach set him on the road to stardom. In addition to his TV show, he now commands hundreds of dollars for a private reading and is booked two years in advance.

Problems with Hot Readings

Although cold reading is the main technique of the new spiritualists, they can also employ "hot" reading on occasion. Houdini (1924) exposed many of these information-gathering techniques, including using planted microphones to listen in on clients as they gathered in the mediums' anterooms—a technique Houdini himself used to impress visitors with his "telepathy." Reformed medium M. Lamar Keene's *The Psychic Mafia* (1976) describes such methods as conducting advance research on clients, sharing other mediums' files (what Keene terms "mediumistic espionage"), noting casual remarks made in conversation before a reading, and so on.

An article in *Time* magazine suggested John Edward may have used just such chicanery. One subject, a marketing manager named Michael O'Neill had received apparent messages from his dead grandfather but, when his segment aired, he noted that it had been improved through editing. According to *Time*'s Leon Jaroff (2001):

> Now suspicious, O'Neill recalled that while the audience was waiting to be seated, Edward's aides were scurrying about, striking up conversations and getting people to fill out cards with their name, family tree and other facts. Once inside the auditorium, where each family was directed to preassigned seats, more than an hour passed before show time while "technical difficulties" backstage were corrected.

Edward has a policy of not responding to criticism, but the executive producer of *Crossing Over* insists: "No information is given to John Edward about the members of the audience with whom he talks. There is no eavesdropping on gallery conversations, and there are no 'tricks' to feed information to John." He labeled the *Time* article "a mix of erroneous observations and baseless theories."

Caught in the Act

Be that as it may, on *Dateline* Edward was actually caught in an attempt to pass off previously gained knowledge as spirit revelation. During the session he said of the spirits, "They're telling me to acknowledge Anthony," and when the cameraman signaled that was his name, Edward seemed surprised, asking "That's you? Really?" He further queried: "Had you not seen Dad before he passed? Had you either been away or been distanced?" Later, playing the taped segment for me, *Dateline* reporter John Hockenberry challenged me with Edward's apparent hit: "He got Anthony. That's pretty good." I agreed but added, "We've seen mediums who mill about before sessions and greet people and chat with them and pick up things."

Indeed, it turned out that that is just what Edward had done. Hours before the group reading, Tony had been the cameraman on another Edward shoot (recording him at his hobby, ballroom dancing). Significantly, the two men had chatted and Edward had obtained useful bits of information that he afterward pretended had come from the spirits. In a follow-up interview Hockenberry revealed the fact and grilled an evasive Edward:

HOCKENBERRY: So were you aware that his dad had died before you did his reading?

Mr. EDWARD: I think he—I think earlier in the—in the day, he had said something.

HOCKENBERRY: It makes me feel like, you know, that that's fairly significant. I mean, you knew that he had a dead relative and you knew it was the dad.

Mr. EDWARD: OK.

HOCKENBERRY: So that's not some energy coming through, that's something you knew going in. You knew his name was Tony and you knew that his dad had died and you knew that he was in the room, right? That gets you . . .

Mr. EDWARD: That's a whole lot of thinking you got me doing, then. Like I said, I react to what's coming through, what I see, hear and feel. I interpret what I'm seeing hearing and feeling, and I define it. He raised his hand, it made sense for him. Great.

HOCKENBERRY: But a cynic would look at that and go, "Hey," you know, "He knows it's the cameraman, he knows it's

DATELINE. You know, wouldn't that be impressive if he can get the cameraman to cry?"

Mr. EDWARD: Absolutely not. Absolutely not. Not at all.

But try to weasel out of it as he might, Edward had obviously been caught cheating: pretending that information he had gleaned earlier had just been revealed by spirits and feigning surprise that it applied to Tony the cameraman. . . .

In his . . . book *Crossing Over*, Edward tries to minimize the *Dateline* exposé, and in so doing breaks his own rule of not responding to criticism. He rebukes Hockenberry for "his big Gotcha! moment," adding:

> Hockenberry came down on the side of the professional skeptic they used as my foil. He was identified as Joe Nickell, a member of the Committee for the Scientific Investigation of Claims of the Paranormal, which likes to simplify things and call itself CSICOP. He did the usual sound bites: that modern mediums are fast-talkers on fishing expeditions making money on people's grief—"the same old dogs with new tricks," in Hockenberry's words.

Edward claims to ignore any advance information that he may get from those he reads, but concedes, "it's futile to say this to a tough skeptic."

Edward may have benefitted from actual information on another occasion, while undergoing a "scientific" test of his alleged powers. In video clips shown, on *Dateline*, Edward was reading subjects—who were brought into the hotel room where he sat with his back to the door—when he impressed his tester with an atypical revelation. Edward stated he was "being shown the movie *Pretty in Pink*" and asked if there was "a pink connection." Then he queried, "Are you, like, wearing all pink?" The unidentified man acknowledged that he was. Yet Edward had thought the subject was a woman, and I suspect that erroneous guess was because of the color of his attire; I further suspect Edward knew it was pink, that as the man entered the room Edward glimpsed a flash of the color as it was reflected off some shiny surface, such as the glass of a picture frame, the lens of the video camera, etc. I challenge Edward to demonstrate his reputed color-divining ability under suitably controlled conditions that I will set up.

Analyzing the Degree of Accuracy

In addition to shrewd cold reading and out-and-out cheating, "psychics" and "mediums" can also boost their apparent accuracy in other ways. They get something of a free ride from the tendency of credulous folk to count the apparent hits and ignore the misses. In the case of Edward, my analysis of 125 statements or pseudostatements (i.e., questions) he made on a *Larry King Live* program (June 19, 1998) showed that he was incorrect about as often as he was right and that his hits were mostly weak ones. (For example he mentioned "an older female" with "an M-sounding name," either an aunt or grandmother, he stated, and the caller supplied "Mavis" without identifying the relationship.)

Another session—for an episode of *Crossing Over* attended by a reporter for *The New York Times Magazine*, Chris Ballard (2001)—had Edward "hitting well below 50 percent for the day." Indeed, he twice spent "upward of 20 minutes stuck on one person, shooting blanks but not accepting the negative responses." This is a common technique: persisting in an attempt to redeem error, cajoling or even browbeating a sitter (as Sylvia Browne often does), or at least making the incorrect responses seem the person's fault. "Do not not honor him!" Edward exclaimed at one point, then (according to Ballard) "staring down the bewildered man."

When the taped episode actually aired, the two lengthy failed readings had been edited out, along with second-rate offerings. What remained were two of the best readings of the show. This seems to confirm the allegation in the *Time* article that episodes were edited to make Edward seem more accurate, even reportedly splicing in clips of one sitter nodding yes "after statements with which he remembers disagreeing."

Edited or not, sessions involving a group offer increased chances for success. By tossing out a statement and indicating a section of the audience rather than an individual, the performing "medium" makes it many times more likely that someone will "acknowledge" it as a "hit." Sometimes multiple audience members will acknowledge an offering, whereupon the performer typically narrows the choice down to a single person and builds on the success. Edward uses just such a technique.

Still another ploy used by Edward and his fellow "psychic mediums" is to suggest that people who cannot acknowledge a hit may find a connection later. "Write this down," an insistent Edward sometimes says, or in some other way suggests the person study the apparent miss. He may become even more insistent, the positive reinforcement diverting attention from the failure and giving the person an opportunity to find some adaptable meaning later.

Presenting the Evidence

Some skeptics believe the way to counter Edward and his ilk is to reproduce his effect, to demonstrate the cold-reading technique to radio and TV audiences. Of course that approach is unconvincing unless one actually poses as a medium and then—after seemingly making contact with subjects' dead loved ones—reveals the deception. Although audiences typically fall for the trick . . ., I deliberately avoid this approach for a variety of reasons, largely because of ethical concerns. . . .

Of course tricking people in order to educate them is not the same as deceiving them for crass personal gain, but to toy with their deepest emotions—however briefly and well intentioned—is to cross a line I prefer not to do. Besides, I believe it can be very counterproductive. It may not be the alleged medium but rather the debunker himself who is perceived as dishonest, and he may come across as arrogant, cynical, and manipulative—not heroic as he imagines.

As well, an apparent reproduction of an effect does not necessarily mean the cause was the same. (For example, I have seen several skeptical demonstrations of "weeping" icons that employed trickery more sophisticated than that used for "real" crying effigies.) Far better, I am convinced, is showing evidence of the actual methods employed, as I did in collaboration with *Dateline NBC*.

Although John Edward was among five "highly skilled mediums" who allegedly fared well on tests of their ability . . .—he did not claim validation on *Larry King Live*. When King (2001) asked Edward if he thought there would ever be proof of spirit contact, Edward responded by suggesting proof was unattainable, that only belief matters: ". . . I think that to prove it is a personal thing. It is like saying, prove God. If you have a belief system and you have faith, then there is nothing really more than that." But this is an attempt to insulate a position and to evade or shift the burden of proof, which is always on the claimant. As Houdini emphatically stated, "It is not for us to prove the mediums are dishonest, it is for them to prove that they are honest." In my opinion John Edward has already failed that test.

Scientific Experiments Do Not Prove Life After Death

Richard Wiseman and Ciaran O'Keeffe

Psychology professor Gary E. Schwartz and his wife, psychologist Linda Russek, recently conducted groundbreaking scientific studies into the possibility of life after death. Actual scientific proof would be a major breakthrough in giving credibility to the paranormal world. It would mean there is finally hard evidence to back up years of claims of an afterlife.

However, scientific proof is not always definitive. In this case, Schwartz and his colleagues were met with much scrutiny from the Committee for the Scientific Investigation of Claims of the Paranormal. Richard Wiseman and Ciaran O'Keeffe, both affiliated with the department of psychology at the University of Hertfordshire in England, decided to investigate Schwartz's study. Wiseman and O'Keeffe found that the study had too many flaws to be considered scientific. They found that Schwartz and his colleagues did not follow the standard procedure for conducting a scientific investigation. More specifically, they did not use blind judging, their control group was inappropriate, and their method of questioning was too broad.

In the following essay Wiseman and O'Keeffe critique Schwartz's investigation.

Schwartz et al.'s first experiment was funded and filmed by a major U.S. television network (Home Box Office—HBO) making a documentary about the survival of bodily death. The study involved two participants (referred to as "sitters") and five well-known mediums. The first sitter was a forty-six-year-old woman who had experienced the death of over six people in the last ten years. Schwartz et al. stated that this sitter was recommended to them by a well-known researcher in ADCs (After Death Communications) who "knew of the sitter's case through her research involving spontaneous ADCs." The second sitter was a fifty-four-year-old woman who had also experienced the death of at least six people in the last ten years.

During the experiment, the sitter and medium sat on either side of a large opaque screen. The medium was allowed to "conduct the reading in his or her own way, with the restriction that they could ask only questions requiring a yes or no answer." Each sitter was asked to listen to the reading and respond to the medium's questions by saying the word "yes" or "no" out loud. The first sitter was given a reading by all five mediums; the second sitter received readings from only two of the mediums.

A few months after the experiment, both sitters were asked to assign a number between -3 (definitely an error) to +3 (definitely correct) to each of the statements made by the mediums. The sitters placed 83 percent and 77 percent of the statements into the +3 category. Schwartz et al. also reported their attempt to discover whether "intelligent and motivated persons" could guess the type of information presented by the mediums by chance alone. The investigators selected seventy statements from the readings given to the first sitter and turned them into questions. For example, if the medium had said "your father loved dancing," the question became "Who loved to dance?" Sixty-eight undergraduates were shown these questions, along with a photograph of the sitter, and asked to guess the answer. Schwartz et al. reported that the average number of items guessed correctly was just 36 percent, and argue that the high level of accuracy obtained by the mediums could not be due to chance guessing.

The first sitter was then invited back to the laboratory to take part in a second experiment. In this experiment she received readings from two of the mediums who also participated in the first study. Rather than being separated by an opaque screen, the sitter sat six feet behind the medium. In the first part of these two readings the sitter was instructed to remain completely silent. In the second part she was asked to answer "yes" or "no" to each of the medium's questions. After reviewing the readings, the sitter rated 82 percent of the mediums' statements as being "definitely correct."

The Schwartz et al. studies suffered from severe methodological problems, namely: (1) the potential for judging bias, (2) the use of an inappropriate control group, and (3) inadequate safeguards against sensory leakage. Each of these problems will be discussed in turn.

Judging Bias

During a mediumistic reading the medium usually produces a large number of statements and the sitter has to decide whether these statements accurately describe his/her deceased friends or relatives. It is widely recognized that the sitter's endorsement of such statements cannot be taken as evidence of mediumistic ability, as seemingly accurate readings can be created by a set of psychological stratagems collectively referred to as "cold reading." It is therefore vital that any investigation into the possible existence of mediumistic ability controls for the potential effect of these stratagems. Unfortunately, the Schwartz et al. study did not contain such controls, and thus it is possible that the seemingly impressive results could have been due to cold reading.

Schwartz et al. reproduced a small part of one reading in their paper, and this transcript can be used to illustrate how cold reading could account for the outcome of the studies. In the first line of the transcript the medium said, "Now, I don't know if they [the spirits] mean this by age or by generation, but they talk about the younger male that has passed. Does that make sense to you?" The sitter answered "yes." The medium's statement is ambiguous and open to several different interpretations. When the medium mentioned the word "younger" he/she could be talking about a young child, a young man, or even someone who died young (e.g., in their forties). The sitters may be motivated to interpret such statements in such a way as to maximize the degree of correspondence with their deceased friends and relatives if, for example, they had a strong belief in the afterlife, a need to believe that loved ones have survived bodily death, or were eager to please the mediums, investigators, and the HBO film crew.

In addition, the sitters may have endorsed the readings because some statements caused them to selectively remember certain events in their lives. As a hypothetical example, let us imagine that the medium had said, "Your son was an extrovert." This statement may have caused the sitter to selectively recall certain life events (i.e., the times that her son went to parties and was very outgoing), forget other events (e.g, the times that he sat alone and didn't want to be with others), and thus assign a spuriously high accuracy rating to the statement.

Biased interpretation of ambiguous statements and selective remembering can lead to sitters endorsing contradictory statements during a reading. Interestingly, the short transcript reproduced by Schwartz et al. contains an example of exactly this happening:

MEDIUM: . . . Your dad speaks about the loss of child. That makes sense?

SITTER: Yes.

MEDIUM: Twice? 'Cause your father says twice.

SITTER: Yes.

MEDIUM: Wait a minute, now he says thrice. He's saying three times. Does that make sense?

SITTER: That's correct.

Some of the statements made by the mediums may also have been true of a great many people and thus had a high likelihood of being endorsed by the sitters. For example, in the transcript the medium stated that one of the spirits was a family member, and elsewhere Schwartz et al. stated that the mediums referred to "a little dog playing ball." It is highly probable that many sitters would have endorsed both of these statements. Research has also revealed that many statements that do not appear especially general can also be true of a surprisingly large number of people. [Researcher Susan] Blackmore carried out a large-scale survey in which more than 6,000 people were asked to state whether quite specific statements were true of them. More than one third of people endorsed the statement, "I have a scar on my left knee" and more than a quarter answered yes to the statement "Someone in my family is called Jack." In short, the mediums in the Schwartz et al. study may have been accurate, in part, because they simply produced statements that would have been endorsed by many sitters.

Other factors may also increase the likelihood of the sitter endorsing the mediums' statements. Clearly, the more deceased people known to the sitter, the greater chance they will have of being able to find a match for the medium's comments. Both sitters knew a relatively large number of deceased people. Both of them had experienced the death of six loved ones in the last ten years, and the first sitter reported that she believed that the mediums had contacted an additional nine of her deceased friends and relatives. Thus, the sitters' high levels of endorsement may have been due, in part, to them having a large number of deceased friends and relatives.

Control Group Biases

Schwartz et al. attempted to discover whether the seemingly high accuracy rate obtained by the mediums could have been the result of chance guesswork. However, the method developed by the investigators was inappropriate and fails to address the concerns outlined above. They selected seventy statements from the readings given to the first sitter in the first experiment and turned them into questions. For example, if the medium had said "your son is very good with his hands," the question became "who was very good with his hands?" These questions were presented to a group of undergraduates, who were asked to guess the answers. Schwartz et al. reported that the average number of items guessed correctly was just 36 percent. However, it is extremely problematic to draw any conclusions from this result due to the huge differences in the tasks given to the mediums and control group. For example, when the medium said, "your son was very good with his hands," the sitter has to decide whether this statement matches the information that she knew about her deceased son. However, as noted above, this matching process may be biased by several factors, including her selective remembering and the biased interpretation of ambiguous statements. For example, the sitter may think back to the times that her son built model airplanes, endorse the statement, and the medium would receive a "hit." However, the control group were presented with a completely different task. They were presented with the question "Who was good with his hands?" and would only receive a "hit" if they guessed that the answer was the sitter's son. They therefore had a significantly reduced likelihood of obtaining a hit than the mediums.

Conceptually, this is equivalent to testing archery skills by having someone fire an arrow, drawing a target around wherever it lands and calling it a bullseye, and then testing a "control" group of other archers by asking them to hit the same bullseye. Clearly, the control group would not perform as well as the first archer, but the difference in performance would reflect the fact that they were presented with very different tasks, rather than a difference in their archery skills.

Psychical researchers have developed various methods to overcome the problems associated with "cold reading" when investigating claims of mediumistic ability. Most of these methods involve the concept of "blind judging." In a typical experiment, a small number of sitters receive a reading from a medium. The sitters are then asked to evaluate both his or her own reading (often referred to as the "target" reading) and the readings made for other sitters (referred to as "decoy" readings). If the medium is accurate then the ratings assigned to the target readings will be significantly greater than those assigned to the decoy readings. However, it is absolutely vital that the readings are judged "blind"— the sitters should be unaware of whether they are evaluating a "target" or "decoy" reading. This simple safeguard helps overcome all of the problems outlined above. Let us suppose that the medium is not in contact with the spirit world, but instead tends to use cold reading to produce seemingly accurate statements. These techniques will cause the sitters to endorse both the target and decoy readings, and thus produce no evidence for mediumistic ability. If, however, the medium is actually able to communicate with the spirits, the sitters should assign a higher rating to their "target" reading than the "decoy" readings, thus providing evidence of mediumistic ability.

It is hoped that future tests of mediumistic ability will employ the type of blind judging methods that have been developed, and frequently employed, in past tests of mediumistic ability.

However, blind judging is only one of several methodological safeguards that should be employed when testing mediumistic ability. Well-controlled tests should also obviously prevent the medium from being able to receive information about a sitter through any normal channels of communication. Unfortunately, the measures taken by Schwartz et al. to guard against various forms of potential sensory leakage appear insufficient.

Sensory Leakage

Throughout all of the readings in the first experiment, and the latter part of the readings in the second experiment, the sitter was allowed to answer "yes" or "no" to the medium's questions. These answers would have provided the mediums with two types of information that may have helped them produce more accurate statements in the remainder of the reading. First, it is very likely that the sitter's voice would have given away clues about her gender, age, and socioeconomic group. This information could cause the mediums to produce statements that have a greater likelihood of being endorsed by the sitter. For example, an older sitter is more likely to have experienced the death of their parents than a younger sitter, and certain life events are gender-specific (e.g., being pregnant, having a miscarriage, etc.). Second, the sitters' answers may have also given away other useful clues to the mediums. For example, let us imagine that the medium stated, "I am getting the impression of someone male, is that correct?" If the sitter has recently lost someone very close to her, such as a father or son, then she might answer a tearful "yes." If, however, the deceased male was an uncle that sitter didn't really know very well, then her "yes" might be far less emotional. Again, a skilled medium might be able to unconsciously use this information to produce accurate statements later in the reading. Any well-controlled test of mediumistic ability should not allow for the sitter to provide verbal feedback to the medium during the reading.

In the first part of the readings in the second experiment, the sitter was asked not to answer yes or no to any of the medium's statements. However, the experimental set-up still employed insufficient safeguards against potential sensory leakage. The medium sat facing a video camera and the sitter sat six feet behind the medium without any form of screen separating the two of them. As such, the sitter may have emitted various types of sensory signals, such as cues from her movement, breathing, odor, etc. Parapsychologists have developed elaborate procedures for eliminating potential sensory leakage between participants. These safeguards frequently involve placing participants in separate rooms, and often the use of specially constructed sound-attenuated cubicles. Schwartz et al. appeared to have ignored these guidelines and instead allowed the sitter to interact with the medium, and/or simply seated them behind one another in the same room. Neither of these measures represent sufficient safeguards against the potential for sensory leakage.

The investigators also failed to rule out the potential for sensory leakage between the experimenters and mediums. The second sitter in the first experiment is described as being "personally known" to two of the experimenters (Schwartz and Russek). The report also described how, during the experiment, the mediums were allowed to chat with Russek in a courtyard behind the laboratory. Research into the possible existence of mediumistic ability should not allow anyone who knows the sitter to come into contact with the medium. Schwartz allowed such contact, with their only safeguard being that the mediums and Russek were not allowed to talk about matters related to the session. However, a large body of research has shown that there are many ways in which information can be unwittingly communicated, via both verbal and nonverbal means. As such, the safeguards employed by Schwartz et al. against possible sensory leakage between experimenter and mediums were insufficient.

In short, the Schwartz et al. study did not employ blind judging, employed an inappropriate control group, and had insufficient safeguards against sensory leakage. As such, it is impossible to know the degree to which their findings represent evidence for mediumistic ability. Psychical researchers have worked hard to develop robust methods for testing mediums since the 1930s. It is hoped that future work in this area will build upon the methodological guidelines that have been developed and thus minimize the type of problems discussed here.

Past-Life Regression Does Not Prove Life After Death

Nicholas P. Spanos

Virginia Tighe helped make past-life regression through hypnosis famous in 1952 when she was hypnotized and began speaking as Bridey Murphy, a nineteenth-century woman from Cork, Ireland. As Bridey Murphy, Tighe was able to recount many details of her life as an Irishwoman. She had many people convinced. Investigators swarmed to Ireland in search of Bridey Murphy. However, traveling out of the country was unnecessary. Bridey Murphy was found to be a neighbor of Tighe's from her childhood. What began as evidence of past lives ended as a vivid imagination.

Even so, past-life regression through hypnosis continued to grow in popularity. If a person in a hypnotic state could remember past lives, it would prove there is life after death. However, critics continue to argue that past-life regression is impossible and that hypnosis only serves to fuel the imagination through suggested imagery from the facilitator. In the

Nicholas P. Spanos, "Past-Life Hypnotic Regression: A Critical View," *Skeptical Inquirer*, vol. 12, Winter 1987–1988, pp. 174–80. Copyright © 1988 by *Skeptical Inquirer*. Reproduced by permission.

following viewpoint, Nicholas P. Spanos argues that those being hypnotized are easily misled by what is real and what is fantasy. He believes that hypnosis cannot prove life after death. Before his death in 1994, Spanos taught psychology.

Some people who have been administered hypnotic-induction procedures followed by suggestions to regress back past their birth times report that they experienced past lives. For instance, a 22-year-old Caucasian woman, while recently "regressed" in our laboratory, claimed that the year was 1940 and that "he" (her past-life identity involved a change of sex) was a Japanese fighter pilot. How are reports of this type to be explained? The parsimonious answer is that they are suggestion-induced fantasy creations of imaginative subjects. If the subjects hold prior beliefs about the validity of reincarnation and/or if they are given encouragement to do so by the hypnotist, they may come to interpret their fantasies as evidence for the existence of actual past-life personalities.

For some, the parsimonious answer will not do. Instead, hypnotically engendered past-life reports are taken as evidence for the validity of reincarnation. Certainly this is the interpretation most commonly conveyed in popular books and articles on the topic. A few mental-health professionals also accept the reincarnation interpretation and even offer past-life therapy to alleviate problems in a client's present life that purportedly stem from unresolved difficulties in some previous incarnation.

Although "hypnosis" has gained a good deal of contemporary scientific legitimation, it continues to be uncritically conceptualized by many as involving profound alterations in consciousness (i.e., the "hypnotic trance state") that produce fundamental changes in perceptual and cognitive functioning. For instance, hypnotic procedures are sometimes seen as enabling subjects to transcend normal volitional capacities (e.g., to eliminate pain, to retrieve "repressed" memories) or as causing subjects to lose voluntary control over mental and behavioral functions (e.g., hypnotically amnesic subjects are supposedly *unable* rather than unwilling to remember). If hypnosis can do all of these remarkable things, then perhaps regression to past lives isn't so farfetched after all. Thus my first concern is to examine what the available experimental data really tell us about the nature of hypnotic phenomena.

Is Hypnosis an Altered State of Consciousness?

After more than a century of research, there is no agreement concerning the fundamental characteristics of the supposed "hypnotic trance state" and there are no physiological or psychological indicators that reliably differentiate between people who are supposedly "hypnotized" and those who are not. Despite widespread belief to the contrary, hypnotic procedures do *not* greatly augment responsiveness to suggestions. Nonhypnotic control subjects who have been encouraged to do their best respond just as well as hypnotic subjects to suggestions for pain reduction, amnesia, age-regression, hallucination, limb rigidity, and so on. Hypnotic procedures are no more effective than nonhypnotic relaxation procedures at lowering blood pressure and muscle tension or effecting other behavioral, physiological, or verbal-report indicators of relaxation. Hypnotic procedures are no more effective than various nonhypnotic procedures at enhancing imagery vividness or at facilitating therapeutic change for such problems as chronic pain, phobic response, cigarette smoking, and so on. In short, the available scientific evidence fails to support the notion that hypnotic procedures bring about unique or highly unusual states of consciousness or that these procedures facilitate responsiveness to suggestions to any greater extent than do nonhypnotic procedures that enhance positive motivation and expectation.

It is important to understand that hypnotic suggestions do not directly instruct subjects to do anything. Instead, suggestions are phrased in the passive voice and imply that something is happening to the subject (e.g., "Your arm is rising," instead of "Raise your arm"). This passive phrasing communicates to subjects the idea that they are supposed to act *as if* the effects suggested are happening automatically. In other words, hypnotic suggestions are tacit requests to become involved in make-believe or *as if* situations. A subject is tacitly instructed to behave as if he is unable to remember, as if his arm is rising, as if he is five years old, and so on. Good hypnotic subjects (*a*) understand the implications of these tacit requests, and (*b*) use their imaginative abilities and their acting skills to become absorbed in the make-believe scenarios contained in suggestions. Thus, by actively using their imaginative abilities, good hypnotic subjects can create and convey the impression that they are unable to remember, unable to lift their "heavy" arms, and so on. The method actor who throws himself into the role of Richard III causes himself to experience the thoughts and emotions that are relevant to his character. Good hypnotic subjects throw themselves into generating the experiences and enactments that are relevant to their roles as hypnotized and as responsive to suggestion.

Age-regression suggestions inform a subject that he is growing younger and younger and returning to an earlier time in his life. Thus a responsive hypnotic subject who is "regressed" to age five states that he is five years old, prints in block letters, and so on. Despite such performances, a good deal of research now indicates that these subjects do *not* in any real sense take on the cognitive, perceptual, or emotional characteristics of actual children. Instead of behaving like real children, age-regressed subjects behave the way they *believe* children behave. To the extent that their expectations about how children behave are inaccurate, their age-regression performances are off the mark. For example, adults commonly overestimate the performance of young children on cognitive and intellectual tasks. Hypnotically age-regressed subjects who are given such tasks usually outperform real children whose ages match those to which the subjects have been regressed.

In short, age-regression suggestions are invitations to become involved in the make-believe game of being a child once again. People who accept this invitation do not, in any literal sense, revert psychologically to childhood. Instead, they use whatever they know about real children, whatever they remember from their own childhood, and whatever they can glean from the experimental test situation to create and become temporarily absorbed in the fantasy situation of being a child. To the extent that their information about childhood is incorrect, their regressed behavior deviates from the behavior of real children.

Hidden Selves

Just as subjects can be given suggestions for age regression, amnesia, or pain reduction, they can also be led to develop the idea that they possess "hidden selves" that they didn't earlier know about. For example, in a number of studies good hypnotic subjects were informed that they possessed "hidden selves" that they were normally unaware of, but who the experimenter could talk to by giving the appropriate signals. When they received these signals, many of these subjects behaved as if they possessed secondary selves that had experiences that differed from those of their "normal selves." When the signals were withdrawn, these subjects often behaved as if they were unable to remember their "hidden self" experiences.

Some investigators interpret such findings to mean that good hypnotic subjects really do carry around unconscious hidden selves with certain intrinsic and unsuggested characteristics. However, a good deal of evidence indicates instead that so-called hidden selves are neither intrinsic to hypnotic procedures nor unsuggested. Quite the contrary, hidden-self performances, like other suggested responses, appear to reflect attempts by motivated and imaginative subjects to create the experiences and role behaviors called for by the instructions they are given. By varying such instructions subjects can be easily led to develop "hidden selves" with whatever characteristics the experimenters wish. Thus, depending upon the instructions they are given, good hypnotic subjects will enact "hidden selves" that report very high levels of pain, very low levels of pain, or both high and low levels of pain in succession. Subjects can also be led to act as if they possess hidden selves that can remember concrete words but not abstract words; or the opposite, hidden selves that see stimuli accurately, see stimuli in reverse, or don't see stimuli at all, and so on.

In short, a subject who behaves as though he possesses a "hidden self," like one who behaves as if he has regressed to age five, is acting out a fantasy. The fantasy performance is usually initiated by the suggestions of the hypnotist, it is imaginatively elaborated upon and sustained by the subject, and (frequently) it earns validating feedback from the experimenter/hypnotist who interacts with the subject as if he or she really did possess a hidden self with particular characteristics.

Past-Life Hypnotic Regression

The few experimental studies that have examined past-life regression have yielded findings that are consistent with the picture of hypnotic responding described above. For example, we . . . completed two experiments on this topic. In the first, 110 subjects were tested for responsiveness to hypnotic suggestions (i.e., hypnotizability). In separate sessions, all of these subjects were individually administered a hypnotic procedure and suggestions to regress to times before their births and then to describe where and who they were. During their individual sessions, 35 subjects enacted past lives. Each subject told the experimenter that he or she was a different person and was living in a different time. Most went on to provide numerous details about where they lived, their past-life occupations, their families, interests, and so on. Subjects who reported past lives scored higher on hypnotizability than those who did not, and were more likely than those who did not to believe that they had experienced some earlier portents of past lives (e.g., déjà vu experiences, dreams).

Among the 35 subjects who reported past lives, there were wide individual differences both in the vividness of the experiences and in the credibility that subjects assigned to them (i.e., the extent to which they believed them to be real past lives as opposed to fantasies). The vividness of past-life experiences was predicted by the subjects' propensity to be imaginative. Thus the frequency with which subjects reported vivid daydreaming and the frequency with which they reported becoming absorbed in everyday imaginative activities (e.g., reading novels) correlated positively with the vividness of their past-life experiences. The best predictor of how much credibility subjects assigned to their past-life experiences was a composite index of their attitudes and beliefs about reincarnation. People who believed in reincarnation, who thought the idea plausible, and who expected to experience past lives assigned higher credibility to their past-life experiences than did those who scored low on this index.

The past-life reporters in our first experiment almost always indicated that their past-life personalities were the same age and race as themselves and usually reported that the past-life personalities lived in Westernized societies. In our second experiment, all subjects were given general information about reincarnation. However, those in one group were further informed that it was not uncommon for people to have been of different sexes or races in past lives and to have lived in exotic cultures. Control-group subjects were given no specific information concerning the characteristics they might expect in their past-life personalities. Among subjects who gave past-life reports, those given the specific information were significantly more likely than controls to incorporate one or more of the suggested characteristics into their past-life descriptions.

The Accuracy of Historical Information

[Researcher H.] Wambach (1979) contended that the historical information obtained from hypnotically regressed past-life responders was almost always accurate. To test this idea in both of our experiments we asked subjects questions that were likely to have historically checkable answers (e.g., Was the responder's community/country at peace or war?). Contrary to Wambach (1979), subjects who gave information specific enough to be checked were much more often incorrect than correct, and the errors were often the type that actual persons from the relevant historical epochs would have been unlikely to make. For example, the "Japanese fighter pilot" described at the beginning of this article was unable to name the emperor of Japan and stated incorrectly that Japan was at peace in 1940. A different subject stated that the year was A.D. 50 and that he was Julius Caesar, emperor of Rome. However, Caesar was never crowned emperor, and died in 44 B.C. Moreover, the custom of dating events in terms of B.C. or A.D. did not develop until centuries after A.D. 50.

[Researchers R.] Kampman and [R.] Hirvonoja (1976) also obtained support for the fantasy-construction hypothesis. After obtaining past-life reports from hypnotic subjects these investigators encouraged subjects to connect various elements of their past-life descriptions with events in their current lives. In this way they often uncovered the sources of information used by subjects to construct their fantasies. We obtained similar findings. For instance, during a post-hypnotic interview, the subject who reported having been Julius Caesar indicated that he was taking a history course and found the section on ancient Rome particularly interesting. Other subjects reported post-hypnotically that, during the previous summer, they had visited the countries where their past-life personalities resided, or suddenly remembered that their past-life wives resembled and had the same names as old girlfriends from their current lives, and so on.

Hypnotic Fantasies

In summary, the available data strongly indicate that past-life reports obtained from hypnotically regressed subjects are the fantasy constructions of imaginative subjects who are willing to become absorbed in the make-believe situation implied by the regression suggestions. Not surprisingly, subjects who responded well to other hypnotic suggestions (high hypnotizables) were also relatively likely to respond to regression suggestions. Moreover, those with the most practice at vivid daydreaming and everyday fantasizing were the ones who created the most vivid past-life fantasies. As do subjects who are asked to regress to childhood, past-life reporters construct their fantasies by interweaving information given in the suggestions with information gleaned from their own life experiences and from what they have read and heard that was relevant to their performances. Moreover, just as age-regressed subjects incorporate misinformation into their enactments of being children, so past-life reporters incorporated historical misinformation into their past-life enactments.

People continually interpret their current experiences in term of established conceptual categories. Consequently, whether people interpreted their past-life experiences as real or imaginary depended upon whether they possessed a belief system that accommodated the notion of real past-lives. Those who believed in reincarnation possessed such belief systems, and therefore were relatively likely to interpret their past-life experiences as veridical rather than imaginary.

Since the classic case of Bridey Murphy, the notion of regression to past lives has been legitimized by common and strongly held misconceptions about the nature of hypnotic responding. A more empirically based conceptualization of such responding that emphasizes its goal-directed nature, its *as if* qualities, and its embeddedness in a nexus of social communications allows past-life enactments to be seen for what they are—interesting and imaginative contextually guided fantasy enactments.

# Epilogue: Analyzing the Evidence

Is life after death fact or fiction? As the articles in this book show, determining the answer is not easy. The subject of life after death is filled with conflict and controversy. The study of life after death is a maze of battling experts and conflicting evidence. Those involved with the subject are passionate about it. You might think that those interested in such a specialized topic would be pleased to work together to solve the great mystery of life after death. However, this is not always the case. For every expert opinion about life after death, there is another that contradicts it. For every piece of evidence that seems sound, some experts say it is not. To further complicate matters, hoaxers are constantly reporting claims of afterlife paranormal activities such as seeing ghosts and communicating with the dead.

Often you may read two or more articles that present very different views of the same topic. How can you tell which view—if either—is telling you the truth? It is sometimes very difficult to decide. That is why it is so important to learn how to read critically, especially when you are reading about controversial topics like the ones in this book.

Reading critically does not mean that you criticize, or say negative things, about an opinion. It means that you analyze and evaluate what you read. You look for clues to decide if an opinion is truthful and reasonable. This epilogue will describe a technique for reading critically and will give you practice in analyzing the articles in this book.

The Author

Perhaps the first thing you should consider is the article's author. Do you know anything about him or her? If you do, this can be an important clue to the article's worth. Does the author have any special qualifications for writing about this subject? Is the author a respected writer known for getting the facts right? Has the author personally made contact with the dead? Is the author a member of a bizarre cult? The answers to these questions can help you decide if the information in the article is worthwhile.

Hypothetical Reasoning

Whether you know anything about the author, you can evaluate an article on its own merits by using hypothetical reasoning. Scientists use hypothetical reasoning to determine if scientific ideas are true. Readers can use hypothetical reasoning to help decide if what they read is fact or fiction. (It is important to recognize that using hypothetical reasoning to analyze an article will not necessarily prove that the author's claims are true. However, if it is done properly, it can determine whether the author has presented a reasonable case in support of his or her claim.)

To use hypothetical reasoning to analyze an article, you will use five steps:

1. State the author's claim (the hypothesis).
2. Gather the author's evidence supporting the claim.
3. Examine the evidence the author uses to support the claim.
4. Consider alternative hypotheses (explanations).
5. Draw a conclusion about the author's claim.

If you have two articles dealing with the same issue (for example, one claims that life after death is fact and the other claims it is fiction), you can apply hypothetical reasoning to both articles. Then, by comparing your analyses, you can see which author has made the strongest case.

One thing to keep in mind is that critically reading one or two articles will help you determine whether those articles are fact or fiction. But it will probably not give you a final answer to the big issue involved. With a topic as controversial and complex as life after death, you will probably have to read many articles and books before you can be confident that you have enough evidence to apply hypothetical reasoning to decide if there is life after death.

In the following sections, we will use hypothetical reasoning to critically examine one of the articles in this book. You can also practice applying the methods to other articles.

1. State the author's claim (the hypothesis).

A hypothesis is a statement that can be tested to determine the likelihood of its truth. To evaluate an article critically, you can start by stating a hypothesis—in this case, a statement of the author's claim. The articles in this book each make claims about life after death, and each article's title alludes to its main claim. The following table shows the major claim of each article, stated as a hypothesis.

One important thing to remember when you write a hy-

Author	Hypothesis
Elisabeth Kübler-Ross	The author's experiences with NDE patients have led her to evidence of an afterlife.
Philip Kapleau	
Leighton Ford	The Bible teaches that heaven exists.
Victor Zammit	Critics use incorrect measures when disproving life after death.
Gary E. Schwartz et al.	Scientific studies show that mediums can communicate with the dead.
Michael Newton	

Author	Hypothesis
Susan Blackmore	People mistake human experiences for scientific evidence of an afterlife.
Hieromonk Seraphim Rose	The Bible explains why reincarnation is not possible.
Paul Kurtz	People forget to look at scientific evidence when they are looking at supernatural phenomena.
Joe Nickell	Psychic mediums are frauds and cannot prove life after death.
Richard Wiseman and Ciaran O'Keeffe	
Nicholas P. Spanos	An overactive imagination can be the result of hypnosis.

pothesis is that it should be a statement that is clear, specific, and provable. Look at the first hypothesis in the table: The author has worked with many patients who have experienced near-death experiences (NDEs). At first glance, this statement might appear clear and specific, but it really is not. What is meant by the term *near-death experience*? This could be many things, from lying in bed with no heart rate to almost falling off a mountain. It is better to state the hypothesis specifically, like the third hypothesis in the table: The Bible teaches that heaven exists. Therefore, let us restate the first hypothesis using more specific language:

Elisabeth Kübler-Ross	The author has witnessed many people at their time of death and has witnessed a similar pattern of events that happen to them just before they die.

Now take a look at the third and last hypotheses in the table. They are problematic because they cannot easily be proved or disproved. They both contain words with ambiguous meanings. What would be the standard for proving that the

Bible is correct in its teaching? Who is to say what is an over-active imagination? These hypotheses should be changed to provable statements. Here is a more provable hypothesis stating Leighton Ford's claim:

Leighton Ford	The author uses the Bible as an expert source that states the existence of heaven.

Read Nicholas P. Spanos's article and see if you can restate his claim in a more provable way:

Nicholas P. Spanos	

Not every author has a provable hypothesis, however. If an article is purely the writer's opinion, you may not be able to state a provable hypothesis.

Also keep in mind that some authors may make several important claims in a single article. To examine the article critically, you will need to state a hypothesis for each important claim.

Hypotheses are not listed for four articles in the long table above. Read the articles and write a clear, specific, and provable statement of the author's main claim for each of these four articles.

Elisabeth Kübler-Ross: "Near Death-Experiences Prove Life After Death"

2. Gather the author's evidence supporting the claim.

Once you have a hypothesis, you must gather the evidence the author uses to support that hypothesis. The evidence is everything the author uses to prove that his or her claim is true. Sometimes a single sentence is a piece of evidence. At other times the evidence consists of a group of several paragraphs. Let us look at the first article in chapter one to see what kind of evidence Elisabeth Kübler-Ross uses to support her claim that she witnessed patients having near-death experiences. The following evidence presents some of Kübler-Ross's evidence:

1. Very close observations of terminally ill patients reveal similar near-death patterns.

2. People were studied from around the world at all age levels and similar denominators about near-death experiences were noted.

3. A study of blind people shows that they can see details of shape, color, and design during an NDE. Their ability to see validates the claim.

3. Examine the evidence the author uses to support the claim.

An author might use many different kinds of evidence to support his or her claims. It is important to recognize different kinds of evidence and to evaluate whether it supports the author's claims. Elisabeth Kübler-Ross uses two main types of evidence, eyewitness testimony and statements of fact. We will look at those now and consider other kinds of evidence later.

Eyewitness testimony. (Item 1 on the evidence list above.) Eyewitness testimony is a type of anecdotal evidence, a story or personal account that may or may not be able to be verified. (This contrasts with hard evidence, which is usually physical evidence or something measurable.) Anecdotal evidence is commonly used as proof of NDEs and other unusual phenomena precisely because hard evidence is so difficult to obtain. An NDE is a personal event, not validated by science. Therefore, anecdotal evidence, especially eyewitness accounts, is often the best evidence available.

Elisabeth Kübler-Ross's whole article is an example of eyewitness testimony. The right eyewitness can provide a great deal of information about an event. However, one thing to keep in mind is that eyewitness reports—of any-thing, not just NDEs—are notoriously unreliable. Because an NDE occurs while the subject is unconscious, much is in-terpreted later when the patient awakens. The patient will remember some details and forget others. And the more time that passes between the actual incident and the time the patient writes a report or is interviewed, the more likely it is that his or her memory will have changed some of the details. In Kübler-Ross's case, she reported findings over sev-eral years. Some of the findings were immediately reported. Others she discovered through surveys and interviews and suffer lapses in time.

You may have seen this common eyewitness exercise en-acted on a television program: A group of people is sitting in a classroom listening to a lecture or doing some other classroom activity. Suddenly a stranger bursts onto the scene. The stranger may "rob" one of the eyewitnesses or do something else dramatic. Then the stranger leaves.

A few moments later, the instructor asks the students to tell what they witnessed. Invariably, different students re-member different things. One remembers that the stranger was of average height and weight; another remembers that he was thin or heavy. One remembers that he had red hair; another remembers that a hood covered his head. One re-members that he was carrying a weapon; another remem-bers that his hands were empty. And so on. When some-thing unexpected happens, especially when it happens quickly or when it evinces great emotion, the mind is not prepared to remember details. This is why independent cor-roborating witnesses—witnesses who remember the same thing and who have not discussed it with each other—can be so important in an investigation.

People in certain occupations are trained to observe events very meticulously, and they are assumed to be better eyewitnesses than the average person. Pilots fit into this classification, as do police officers. The fact that Kübler-Ross is a doctor trained to observe and listen to patients gives her credibility. In fact, she states that when she began practicing medicine, she had no preconceived notions of what happens when we die. Her experiences with dying patients, through careful observations, drew her to definitive conclusions.

Another factor in evaluating eyewitness articles is the witness's reputation. Does the witness (Kübler-Ross, in this case) have a reputation for honesty? publicity-seeking? exaggeration? scholarship? flakiness? The introduction to Kübler-Ross's article tells you that she is known for her devotion to her patients. It also states that she began as a skeptic, and through years of research changed her beliefs. The fact that she is a doctor helps her credibility.

Bias must also be eliminated when evaluating an eyewitness report. *Bias* refers to preconceived ideas about something. In other words, an eyewitness report can be affected by the witness's past experience, by other things he or she knows, by personal prejudice, and other factors. For example, NDEs are more accepted by New Age groups than by those in a scientific field. NDEs have not been scientifically linked to proof of life after death, even though an overwhelming majority of those having experienced an NDE believe it to be proof of life after death. Kübler-Ross is in a unique situation because she is a doctor who entered the field of study as a skeptic with a scientific bias and has now become a strong believer based on her experiences. So, it seems safe to say that Kübler-Ross's article was without bias.

What do you think? Considering the information in this section, does Elisabeth Kübler-Ross appear to be a good eyewitness? Do her personal experiences with dying patients support her claim that NDEs are proof of life after death?

Statement of fact. A statement of fact presents information as being true. "Elisabeth Kübler-Ross is a doctor" is a statement of fact. It is stated as a truth, and it can be verified. Beware of statements that look like facts but cannot be confirmed: "When we leave the physical body there will be a total absence of panic, fear, or anxiety" is stated as though it were a fact, but we do not know for sure that it is true.

Ideally, to significantly support an author's claims, the statements of fact that he or she uses should be verifiable. They should be something you can look up in an encyclopedia or other reference book. Or the author should tell you the source of the information so that you can confirm it. Or the statements of fact should be something you can test to find out if they are true. However, many authors expect you to accept their statements of fact as true just because they tell you so. Be careful about accepting facts just because the author states them. Look for corroborating evidence (evidence that helps confirm the truth).

Look again at the evidence list for Kübler-Ross. Which of Kübler-Ross's statements of fact can be verified, and which cannot?

Now we must consider whether Kübler-Ross's statements of fact support the hypothesis that her experiences with NDE patients have led her to evidence of an afterlife. What do you think?

4. Consider alternative hypotheses (explanations).

An important step in critically examining an article is to consider whether the author considers other explanations that might fit his or her facts. If the author considers only one explanation that might mean that he or she is presenting a biased, or one-sided, view or that he or she has not fully considered the issue.

Occam's Razor is a famous principle used when considering claims of the unusual. The principle states that the simplest explanation is probably the best. In other words, if the evidence can be explained by something ordinary, there is no reason to look for unusual or exotic explanations. Thus, the critical reader has to determine whether the author has considered other explanations and if he or she has looked for common explanations that will fit the evidence as well as an exotic explanation does.

With life after death, common explanations that should be examined include eyewitness testimony, shared experiences, and psychical phenomena. For example, most ghost investigations stem from eyewitness testimony. The more eyewitnesses that see the ghost, the more valid the ghost becomes.

However, eyewitness accounts alone do not prove anything. For example, several people could witness a ghost in a graveyard. To the average person it may seem clear that what he or she sees is a ghost. However, scientific investigation could prove a logical explanation such as phosphorescence illuminating a gravesite.

Does Kübler-Ross consider common explanations against claims of life after death? Kübler-Ross's entire study is based on common explanations in support of life after death, mainly through eyewitness testimony. It is through thousands of testimonials that Kübler-Ross bases her beliefs. Through these testimonies and her earlier skepticism, Kübler-Ross does examine opposing views. For example, Kübler-Ross examines the possibility of near-death experiences as proof of life after death being the result of wishful thinking. However, Kübler-Ross concludes that wishful thinking is not responsible for the cases she has studied due to two reasons. The fact that most cases were the result of sudden, unexpected accidents disproves the theory of wishful thinking. Patients did not have time to ponder their fate. The second explanation involves the study of blind people who have had near-death experiences. Kübler-Ross states that blind people "would not be able to share with us the color of a sweater, the design of a tie, or many details of shape, color, and designs of people's clothing." In fact, she states that in her study blind people were able to accurately describe many details of all the people present at the time of their passing. Do you believe this is sufficient evidence to prove life after death?

As a critical reader, you should consider information that is not in the author's article as well. For example, Kübler-Ross focuses on personal experiences and her studies to prove life after death. Could she be missing something? Susan Blackmore thinks she is. Blackmore's article, "Near-Death Experiences are Not Proof of Life After Death," charges there are scientific explanations to each of Kübler-Ross's claims. For example, Kübler-Ross believes those who experience an NDE have common experiences. One experience that she describes is passing though a tunnel towards a bright light. Blackmore suggests in her article that the light can be explained scientifically. She believes during an NDE the cortex of the brain allows one to only see clearly a center field of vision, which is described as a tunnel. Should Kübler-Ross examine scientific studies such as Blackmore's hypothesis before drawing her own conclusions?

5. Draw a conclusion about the author's claim.

Finally, after considering the evidence and alternative explanations, it is time to make a judgment, to decide if the hypothesis makes sense. You can tally up the evidence that does and does not support Kübler-Ross's claim and see how many pros and how many cons you have. But that is really too simple. You will have to give more weight to some kinds of evidence than to others. For example, almost all of Kübler-Ross's evidence is based on her observations, which may be entirely accurate, but it cannot be verified by any objective means. What do you think—does Elisabeth Kübler-Ross adequately support her claim that her experiences with NDE patients are proof of an afterlife?

Other Kinds of Evidence

Here are some additional types of evidence authors commonly use to support their claims.

Celebrity or expert testimonial. Many writers support their claims with testimony from a celebrity or an expert. A lot of television ads do this. You have probably seen the GAP commercials that have popular entertainers singing while wearing GAP jeans, and you have seen commercials for aspirin and other medicines that have a doctor praising the medicine. Advertisers know that many people are influenced when a celebrity or an expert says something is true.

Celebrity testimony usually does not have much value as evidence: If a celebrity wears a certain brand of jeans, does it mean the jeans are good quality? If an automobile commercial shows a famous architect looking at a car and saying that he likes to look at beautiful things, does that mean the car is a well-built, reliable vehicle?

Expert testimony can provide valuable evidence, however. For example, psychiatrists, psychologists, and other doctors in this field can evaluate hypnotism as a means of communicating with a former life. An expert will be able to determine a person's state of mind under hypnosis or the subject's degree of reality. The expert, however, does need to be an expert of the topic to be considered. A biology expert cannot necessarily provide important information about metal composition.

An author who uses expert testimony should provide sufficient information for readers to judge whether that person is qualified on the topic.

Statistical evidence. Authors sometimes use statistics or

other numerical data to support their claims. For example, they may cite a survey or state that a certain percentage of people have observed apparitions. Be sure to carefully evaluate numerical claims. Just because a large number of people claim to have seen apparitions does not prove that they saw a ghost. Also pay attention to where the author obtained the information. For example, information from the Psychical Research Center is going to be more reliable than an individually run website about ghosts.

When analyzing statistical evidence, consider the following: When was the survey conducted? (Was it in 1919? 1950? 1999? Our knowledge of life after death has changed over the years, and the answers would reflect the knowledge of the time.) Who conducted it? (Was it an independent polling organization such as the Gallup Group? Was it psychic buffs? Ghost hunters? Each group would have its own biases that could influence the survey.) How many people were surveyed, and who were they? (It makes quite a difference whether a dozen people or a thousand were surveyed! And it makes a lot of difference if the people were doctors or part of a life-after-death fan club, volunteers, or part of a scientifically selected group. Volunteers tend to have a particular interest in the topic being studied, so their views may not be typical of the general population. Professional pollsters know how to select participants so that they represent a true cross-section of the population, representing people of different ages, races, educational backgrounds, and so on.) The survey's questions and the way they are phrased can also affect the survey's results.

Logical fallacy. Logic comes from the Greek word for reason. *Logical thinking* means to reason things out. (Hypothetical reasoning is a form of logical reasoning.) A logical fallacy is when logical reasoning fails. You think you are reasoning logically, but you are not.

A generalization can be an example of a logical fallacy:

I have never seen a ghost, therefore, ghosts do not exist.

Another type of logical fallacy makes a false analogy. That is, it wrongly compares two items based on a common quality. Here is an example:

Honeybees make honey. Honeybees have yellow stripes. Wasps also have yellow stripes, so wasps must make honey.

The fallacy is that yellow stripes have nothing to do with the ability to make honey, so the argument falls apart.

Here is another example:

The witness saw an unknown shape moving throughout the house. Ghosts are unknown shapes, so the witness must have seen a ghost.

This fallacy is twofold: First, many things are of unknown shape. The witness could have seen anything, from a clothes tree to another person. Second, no one knows for sure what a ghost—if they do exist—looks like; witnesses have reported many different shapes.

Physical evidence. In some cases, there is physical evidence when studying life after death. This might include brain wave activity at the time of death or photographic evidence of ghosts. If an article describes physical evidence, it should tell how the evidence was investigated. Generally, a qualified investigator (someone who knows how to collect evidence without contaminating it) will photograph the evidence in place and then take samples to be analyzed in a lab—or, preferably, in two or more independent laboratories.

Depending on the type of evidence, a laboratory can analyze it for chemical makeup, cell damage or mutation, magnetism, radiation, and various other things. The aim will be to discover if there is anything unusual about the sample.

When a witness is able to take a photo or video of a ghost, the challenge is proving that the film is undoctored and that it does not simply show something normal in an unusual light. This challenge has become ever greater as technology has become more and more sophisticated and inexpensive. A couple of decades ago, if you had the original negative, a doctored film was fairly easy to discover. A really good fake could only be made with rare and expensive photographic equipment. Today, with computers and digital cameras readily available, it has become fairly easy for people without special skills to make a fake photo or video, and some of these are extremely difficult to detect without the help of experts with sophisticated equipment.

Read the article "Life After Death Theories Are Provable" by Victor Zammit. Does the author tell how the evidence was examined? How it was analyzed and by whom? Were the analyzers experts qualified to do this kind of analysis? Does the physical evidence described in this article prove life after death? Explain.

Now You Do It!

Choose one article from this book that has not already been analyzed and use hypothetical reasoning to determine if the author's evidence supports the hypothesis. Here is a form you can use:

Name of article_____ Author_____

1. State the author's hypothesis.

2. List the evidence.

3. Examine the evidence. For each time listed under number 2, state what type of evidence it is (eyewitness testimony, statement of fact, etc.) and evaluate it: Does it appear to

be valid evidence? Does it appear to support the author's hypothesis?

4. Consider alternative hypotheses. What alternative explanations does the author consider? Does he or she examine them fairly? If the author rejects them, does the rejection seem reasonable? Are there other alternative explanations you believe should be considered? Explain.

5. Draw a conclusion about the hypothesis. Does the author adequately support his or her claim? Do you believe the author's hypothesis holds up under scrutiny? Explain.

For Further Research

Books

Loyd Auerbach, *Psychic Dreaming: A Parapsychologist's Handbook*. New York: Barnes and Noble, 1999.

John Edward, *Crossing Over: The Stories Behind the Stories*. San Diego: Jodere Group, 2001.

Philip Kapleau, *The Wheel of Life and Death: A Practical and Spiritual Guide*. New York: Bantam Doubleday, 1989.

Elisabeth Kübler-Ross, *On Life After Death*. Berkeley, CA: Celestial Arts, 1991.

Joel Martin and Patricia Romanowski, *We Don't Die: George Anderson's Conversations With the Other Side*. New York: Berkeley, 1989.

Melvin Morse, *Where God Lives: The Science of the Paranormal and How Our Brains Are Linked to the Universe*. New York: HarperCollins, 2000.

Melvin Morse and Paul Perry, *Closer to the Light: Learning from Children's Near-Death Experiences*. New York: Villard Books, 1990.

Michael Newton, *Destiny of Souls: New Case Studies of Life Between Lives*. St. Paul: Llewellyn Publications, 2000.

Massimo Polidoro, *Final Séance: The Strange Friendship Between Houdini and Conan Doyle*. Amherst, NY: Prometheus Books, 2001.

Hieromonk Seraphim Rose, *The Soul After Death*. Platina, CA: Saint Herman of Alaska Brotherhood, 1982.

Gary E. Schwartz, *The Afterlife Experiments*. New York: Pocket Books, 2002.

Helen Wambach, *Reliving Past Lives: The Evidence Under Hypnosis*. New York: Barnes and Noble, 1978.

Periodicals

Loyd Auerbach, "Psychic Frontiers," *FATE Magazine*, April 1998.

Susan Blackmore, "Near-Death Experiences: In or Out of the Body?" *Skeptical Inquirer*, 16, 34–35, 1991.

Perry DeAngelis and Steven Novella, "Hunting the Ghost Hunters," *Connecticut Skeptic*, Summer 1997.

Brendan J. Koerner, "Near-Death Experiences May Be Physiological. Or They May Be Peepholes into a World Beyond," *U.S. News & World Report*, March 31, 1997.

Paul Kurtz, "The New Paranatural Paradigm: Claims of Communicating with the Dead," *Skeptical Inquirer*, November/December 2000.

Ruth LaFerla, "A Voice from the Other Side," *New York Times*, October 29, 2000.

Joe Nickell, "John Edward: Hustling the Bereaved," *Skeptical Inquirer*, November/December 2001.

Nicholas P. Spanos, "Past-Life Hypnotic Regression: A Critical View," *Skeptical Inquirer*, Winter 87–88.

Richard Wiseman and Ciaran O'Keeffe, "A Critique of Schwartz et al.'s After-Death Communication Studies," *Skeptical Inquirer*, November/December 2001.

Internet Sources

Allen Botkin, *Induced ADC's*, Business Writing Center, 2002. www.induced-adc.com.

Comparing U.S. Religious Beliefs with Other "Christian" Countries, Ontario Consultants on Religious Tolerance, 2003. www.religioustolerance.org.

Leighton Ford, *Preaching Today Tape #96*, Christianity Today International, 2003. www.preachingtoday.com.

The Fox Sisters and Modern Spiritualism, Wayne County Historical Society, 2001. www.members.aol.com/wchs4943history.

Bill and Judy Guggenheim, *After-Death Communication: Joyous Reunions with Deceased Loved Ones*, The ADC Project, 2000. www.after-death.com.

Induced ADC's for Grief Therapy, Business Writing Center, 2002. www.induced-adc.com.

Bruce Daniel Kettler, *The New Age*, 1997. www.psicounsel.com.

The Natural Death Handbook, Chapter 3, Near Death Experiences, Natural Death Centre, 1993. www.globalideasbank.org.

Matt Nesbit, *Talking to Heaven Through Television: How the Mass Media Package and Sell Psychic Medium John Edward*, 2001. www.csicop.org.

Gary Nurkiewicz, *Psychotherapy, Astrological Counseling, and Past Life Regression Therapy*. www.transformystic.com.

Karlis Osis, *Life After Death?*, American Society for Psychical Research, 2001. www.aspr.com.

Passages Through Time: Past Life and Afterlife Regressions to Discover Your Soul's Purpose, Subconscious-Solutions, 2002. www.passagesthroughtime.com.

Steve Richards, *Immortality and Life After Death Problems*, 2002. www.faithnet.freeserve.co.uk.

Kevin Williams, *The Secret World of Dreams: A Connection to the Afterlife*, Near-Death Experiences and the Afterlife, 2003. www.near-death.com.

Winston Wu, *Debunking Common Skeptical Arguments Against Paranormal and Psychic Phenomena*, 2001. www. survivalscience.org.

Victor Zammit, *A Lawyer Presents the Case for the Afterlife: Irrefutable Objective Evidence*, 2000. www.victorzammit. com.

Index

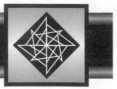